Collecting words

(VERY) **SHORT**
(VISUAL) **STORIES**

BRIAN FOUHY

FOREWORD

About five years ago I was introduced to Instagram. As a result, like many, I started to take more pictures, become more aware of my surroundings, and began to realize photographs are all aro und us. As a visual person who enjoys a good word, signage and graffiti began to catch my eye, and became a focus of my photography.

Wherever I go, I always make an effort to wander and explore to see what I can find. I most enjoy getting "lost" which is where things can get interesting. The words I seem to like best are the ones I don't see coming, which I'll sometimes pass only to realize after continuing down the road for a few minutes that I need to track back and get the word. I feel this happens for two reasons: it encourages me to actively live in the moment because who knows if I will ever be back to wherever I am to get that photo or word again. I have also learned through this experience that words and objects in the world are more ephemeral than we realize. We often think we'll catch it next time. However, I have returned to places that I have previously found some of my favorite words, only to find they no longer exist. While it is bittersweet that they have disappeared, I enjoy knowing what was once there.

As my collection of words began to grow, I started wondering if stories could be created by combining the photos. I began merging together the words based on their intended meaning mixed with both the meaning they take on from their environment, and the way they are presented, to create a unique narrative. The last few years of wandering and exploring has allowed me to amass well over 500 photos, which has provided me the volume of words to attempt to create these stories. You will find the outcome on the following pages.

The words we see, are the words we read.

IT WOULDN'T FLUSH

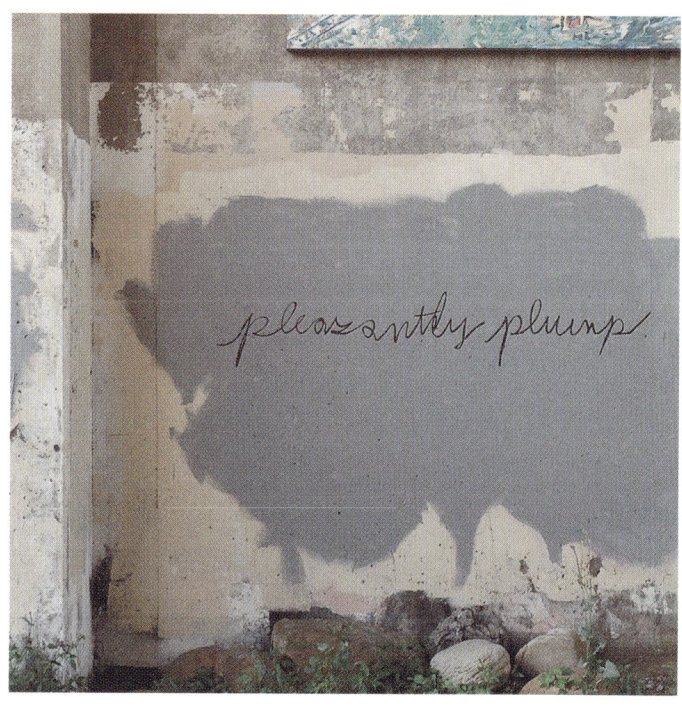

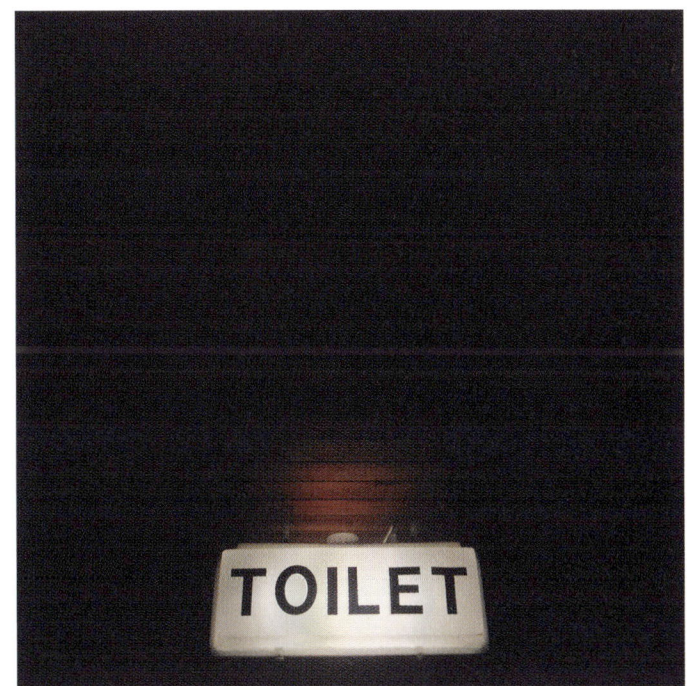
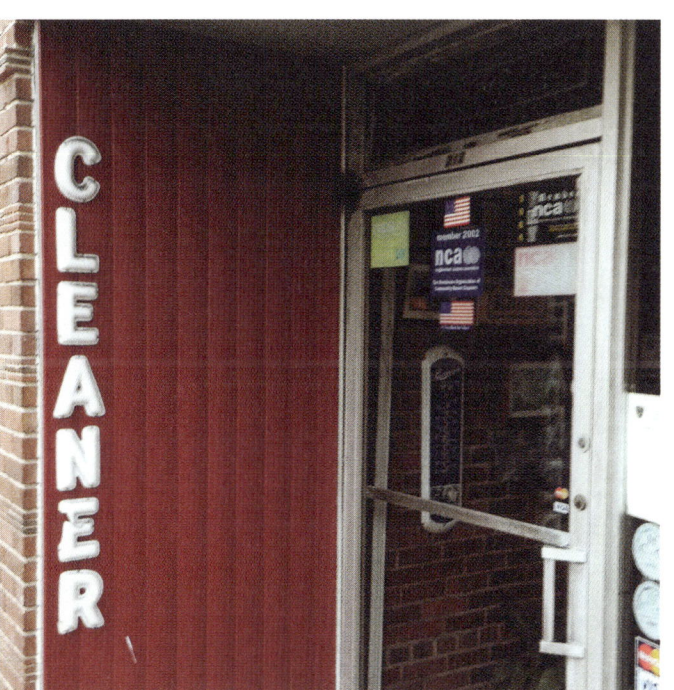

FRANKS & BEANS

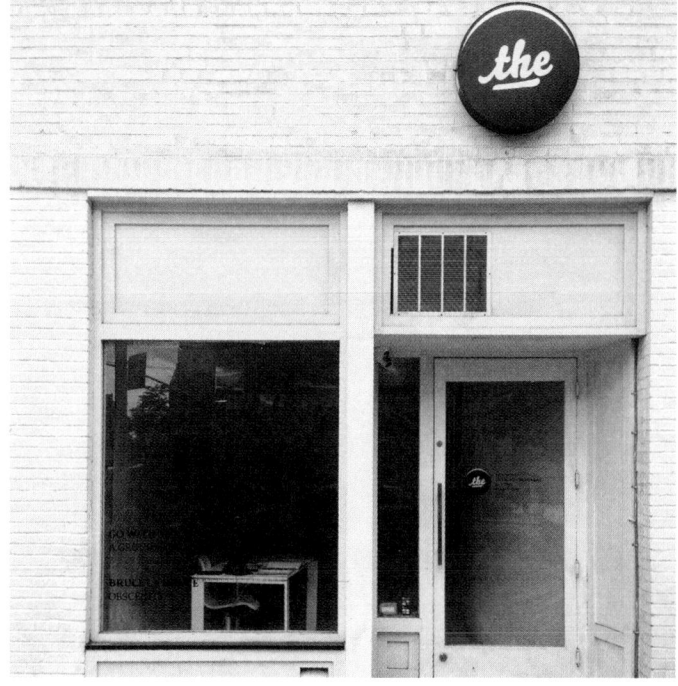

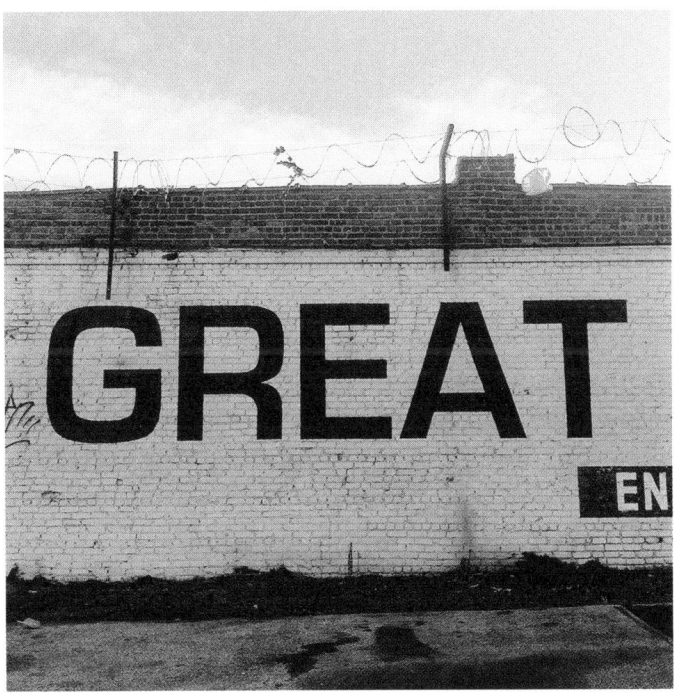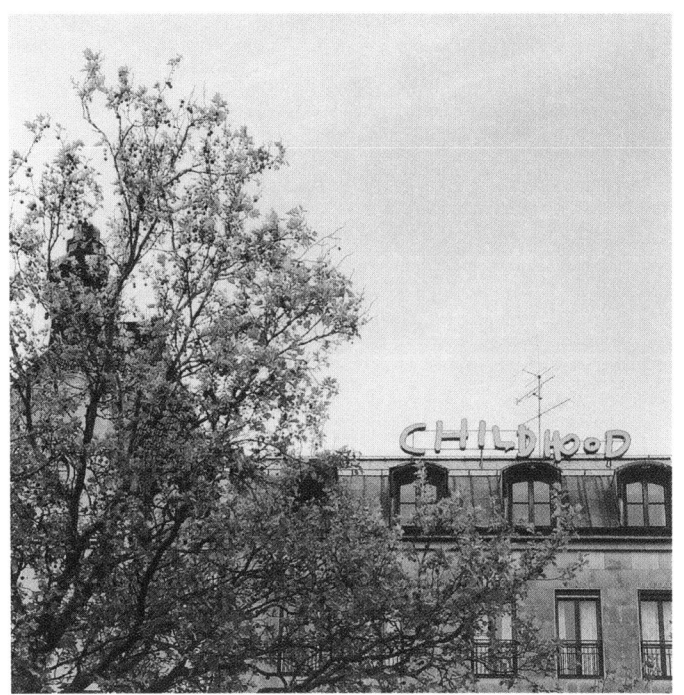

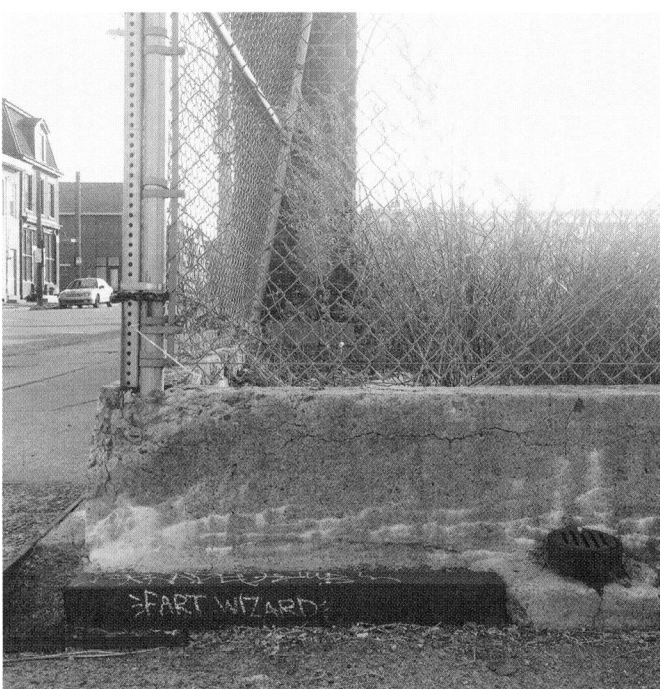

KNOCK TWICE

ASK FOR BOB

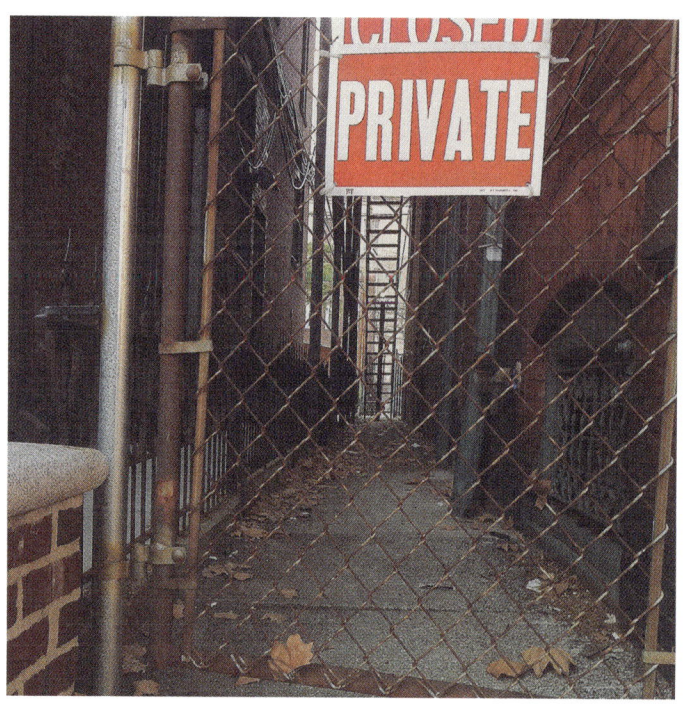

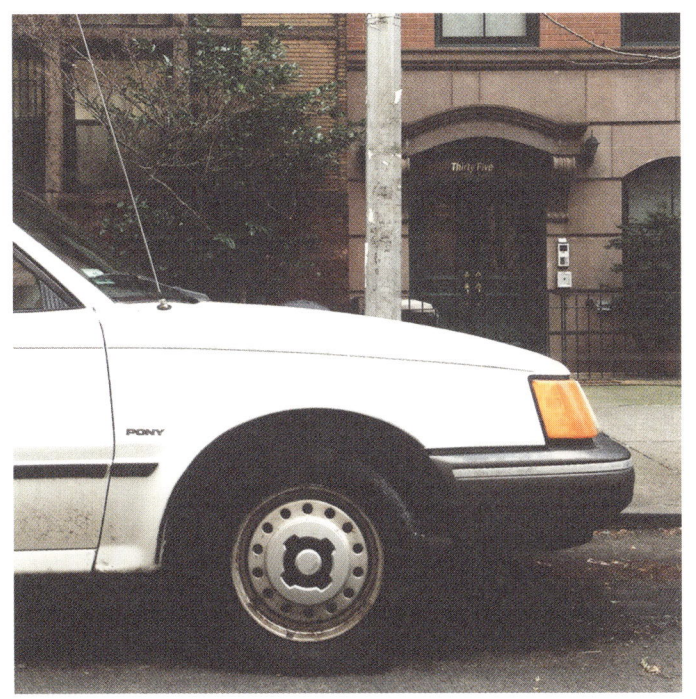
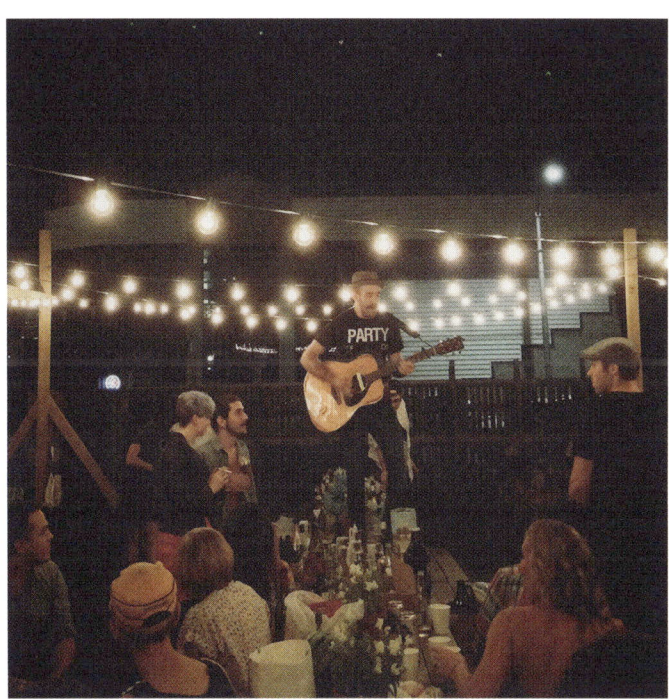

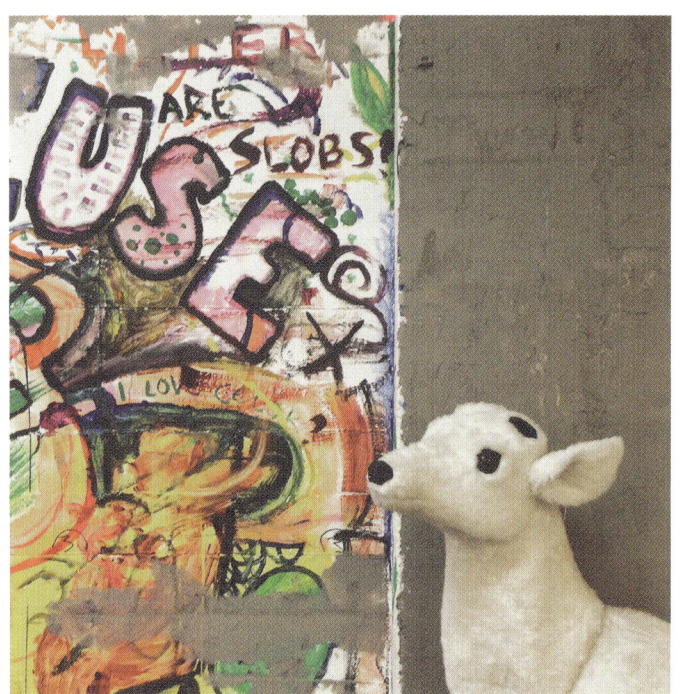
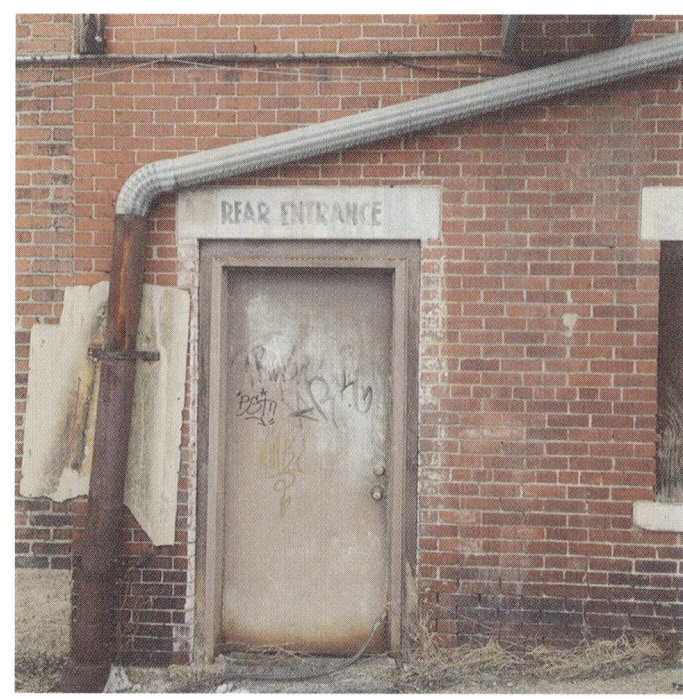

SEE ME AFTER CLASS

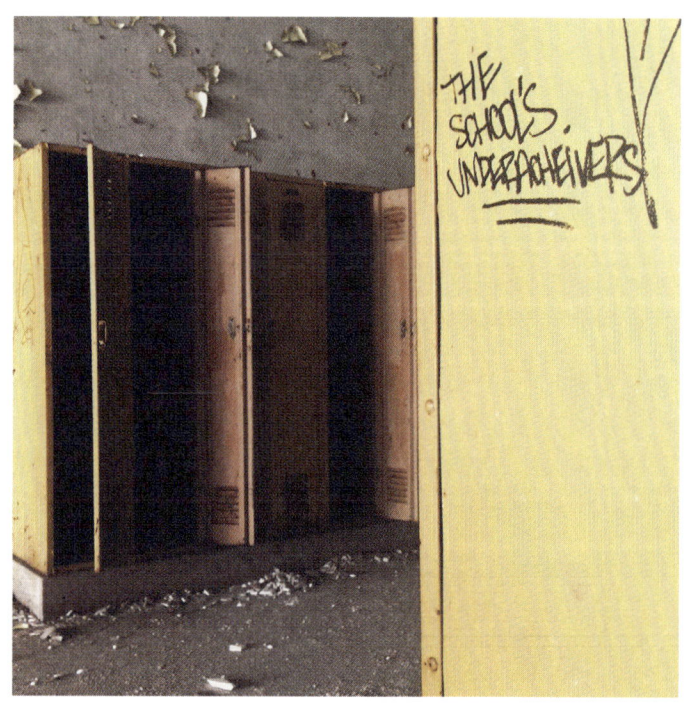

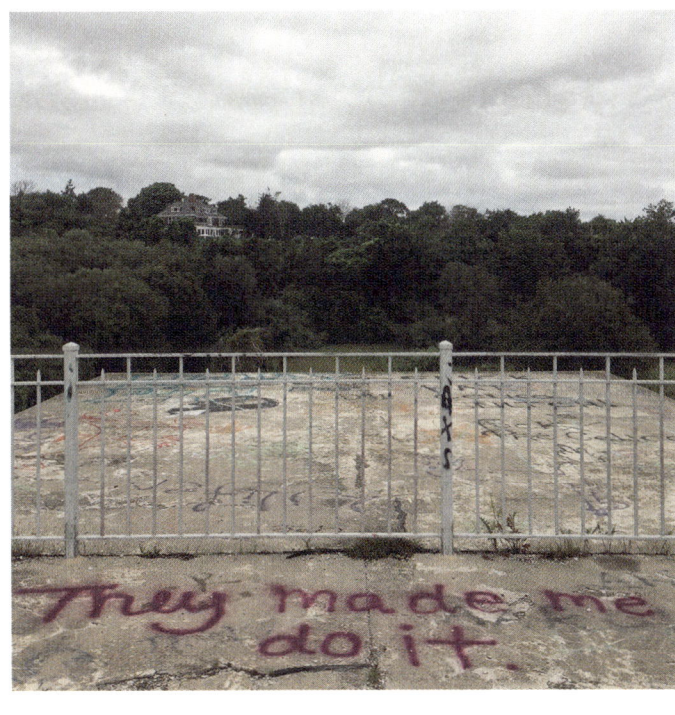

FAT & LAZY

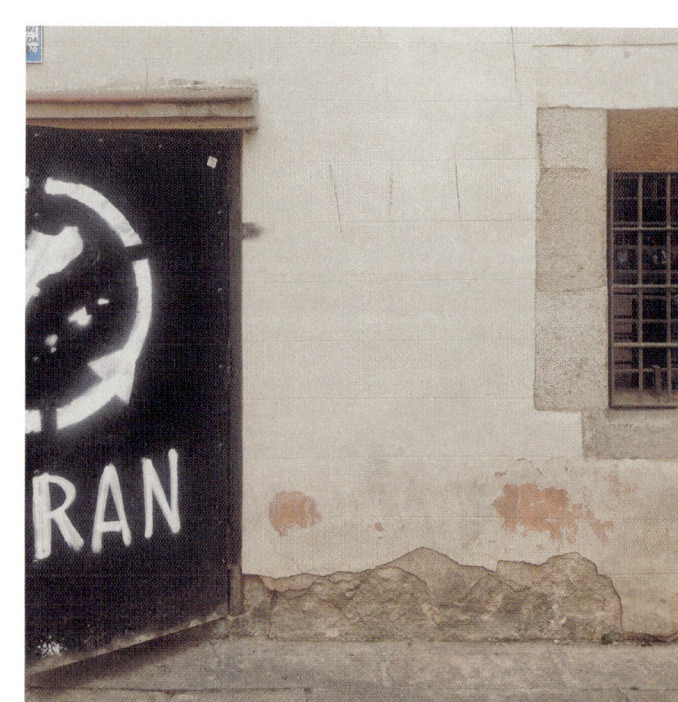

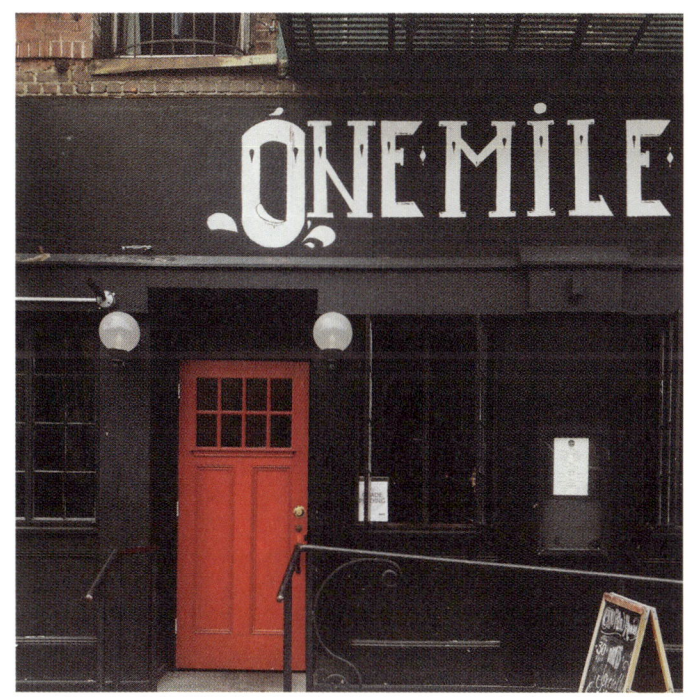
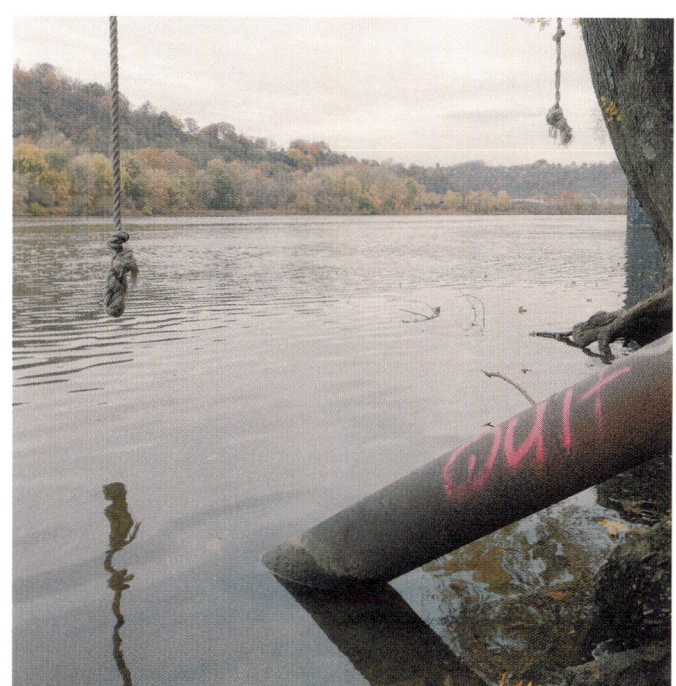

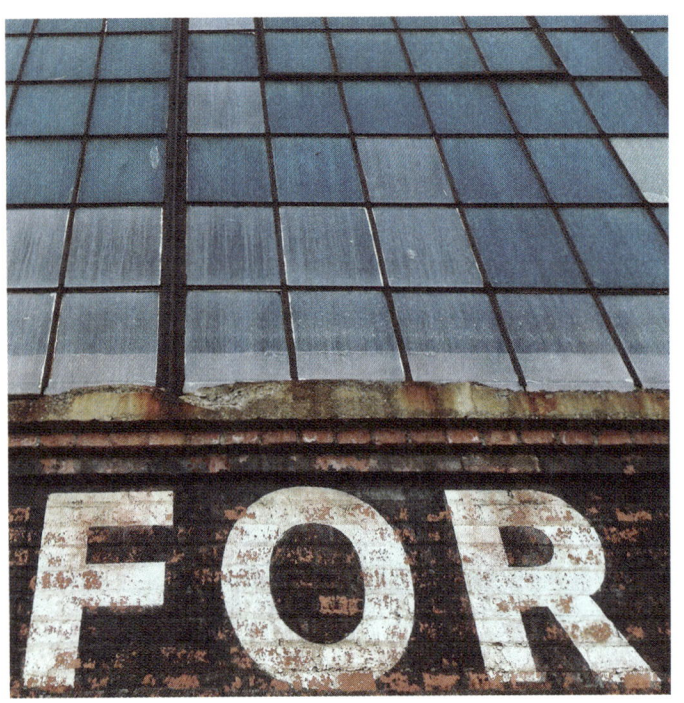
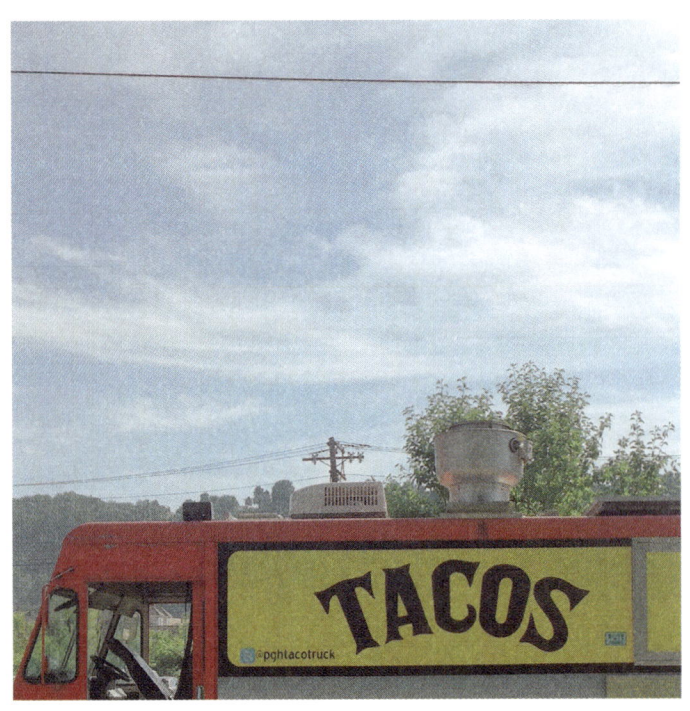

SHOTGUN

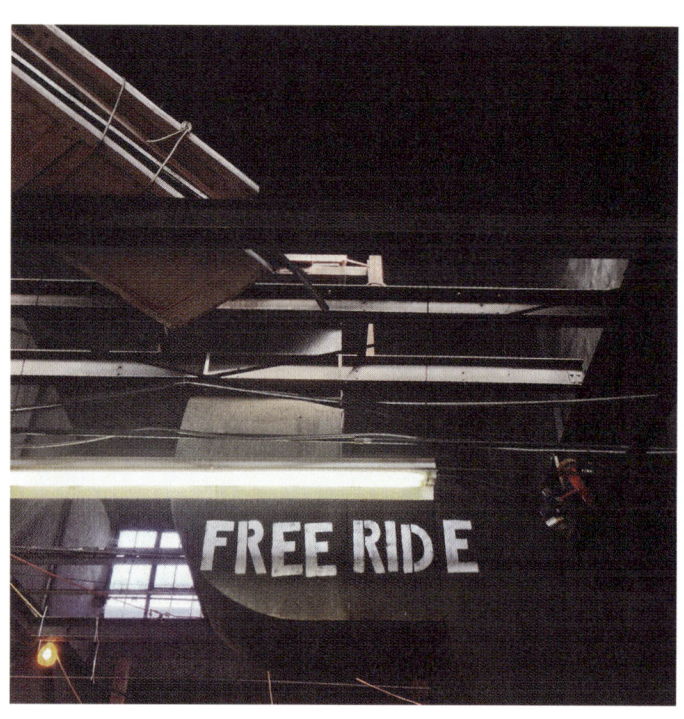

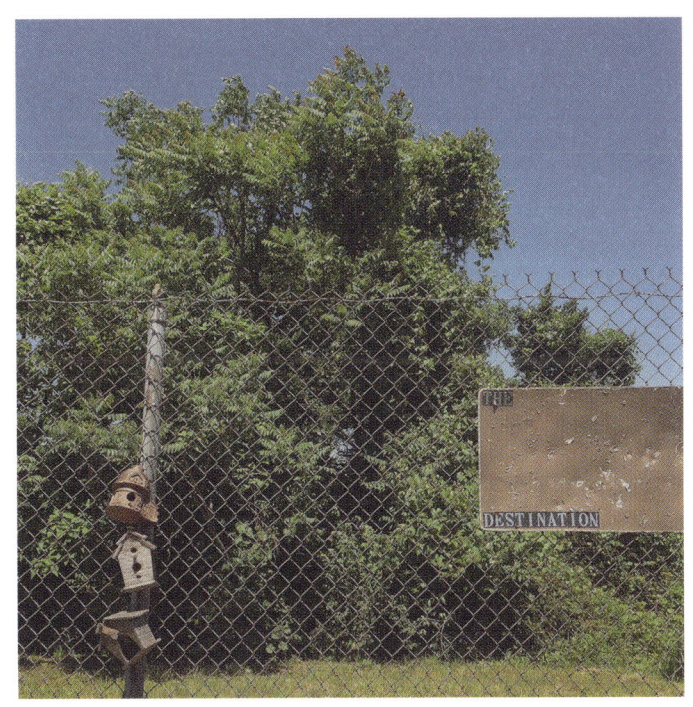

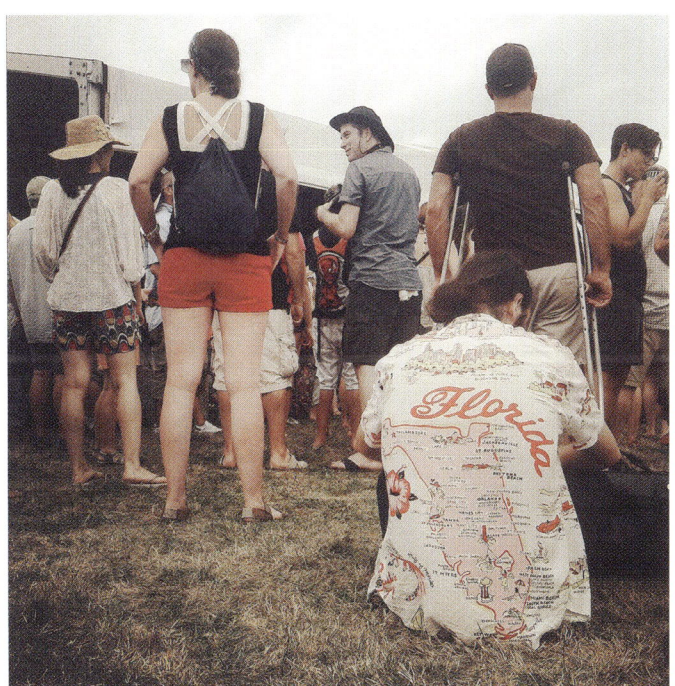

WHEN I GROW UP

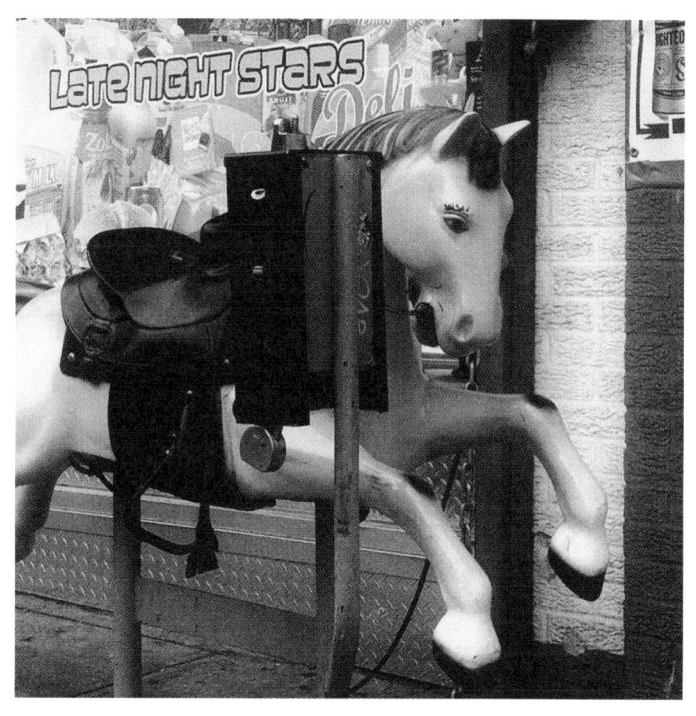

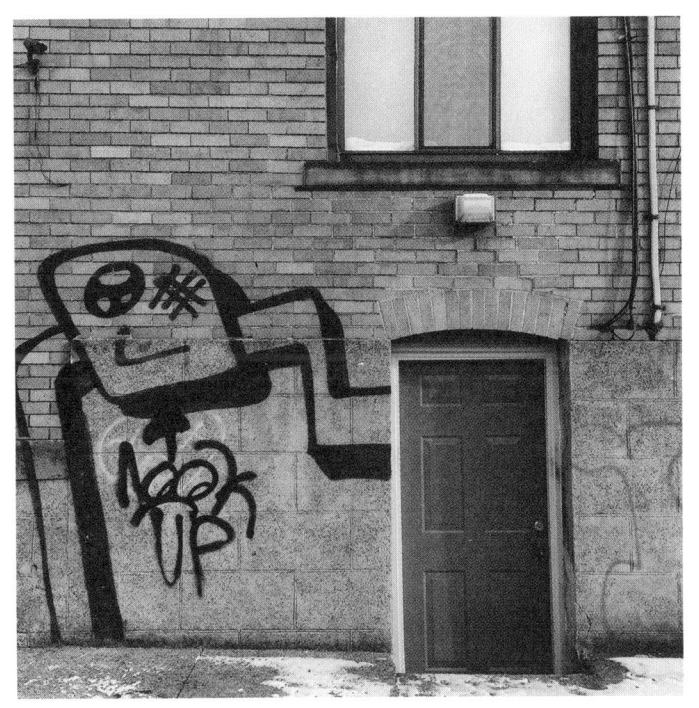
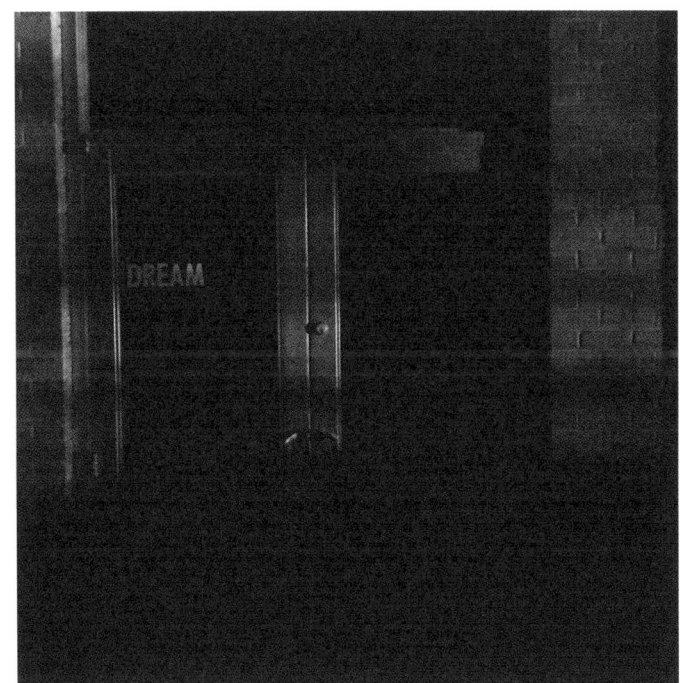

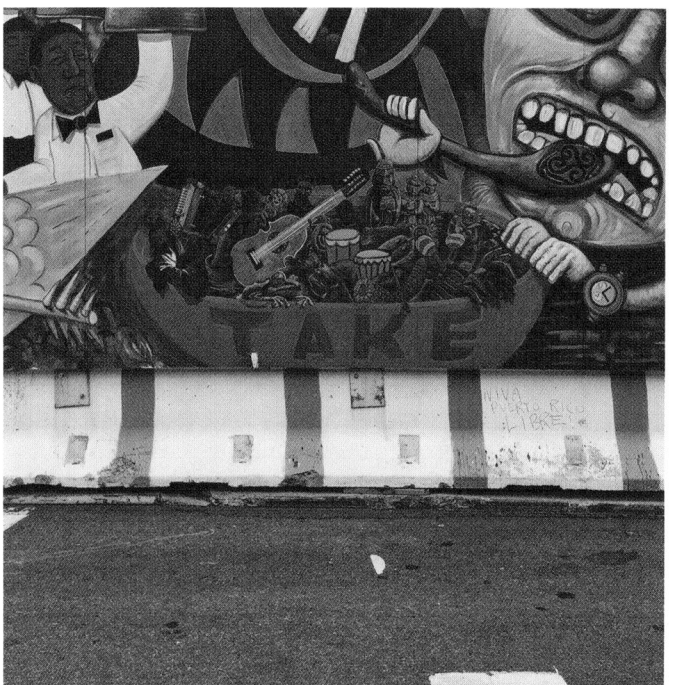
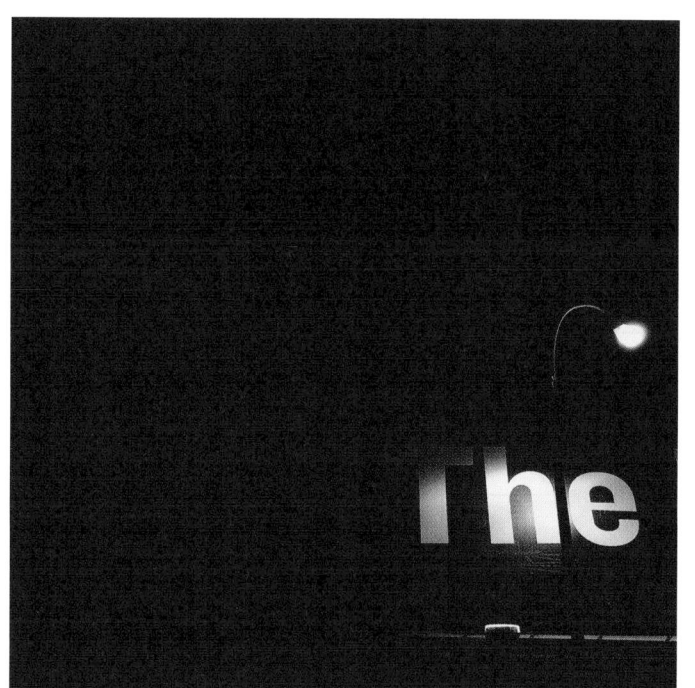

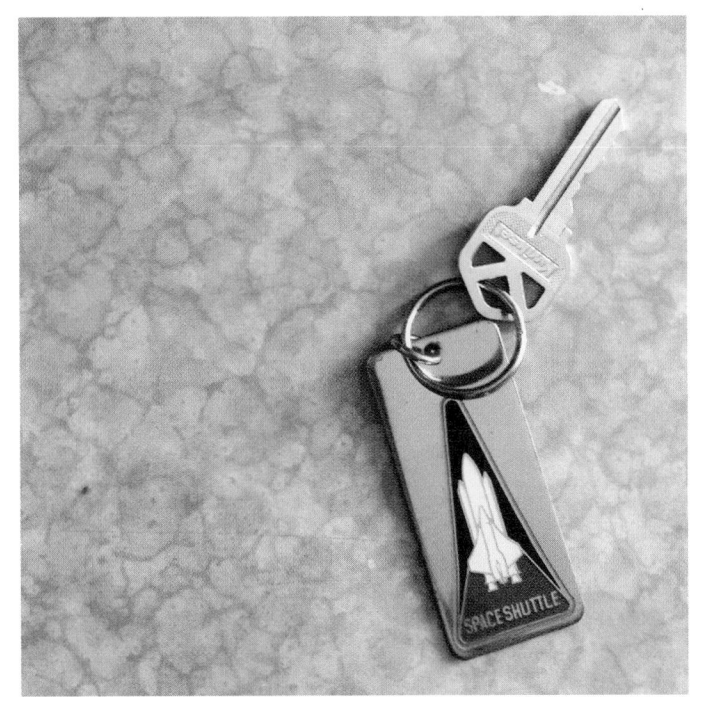
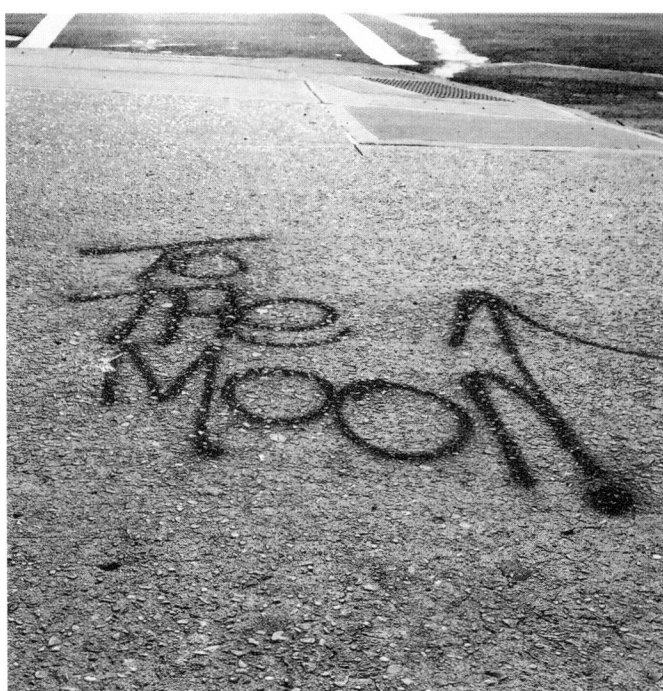

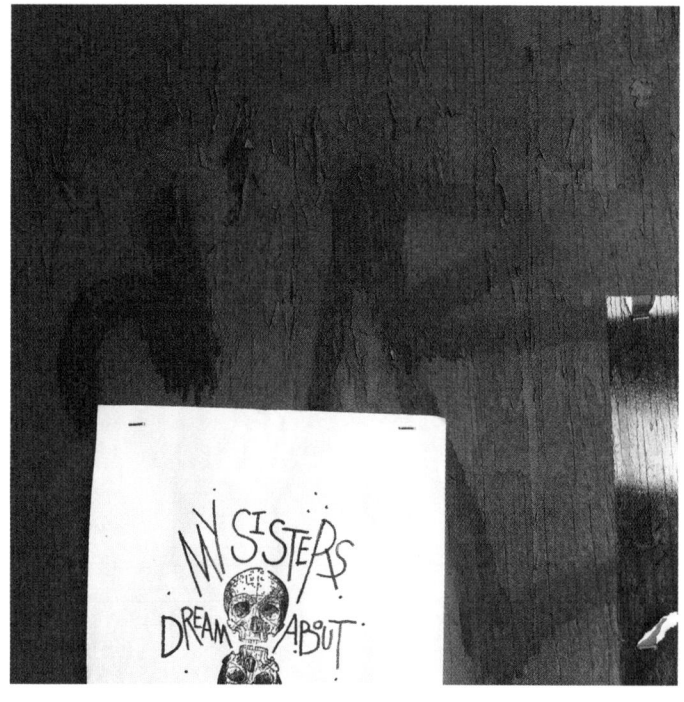

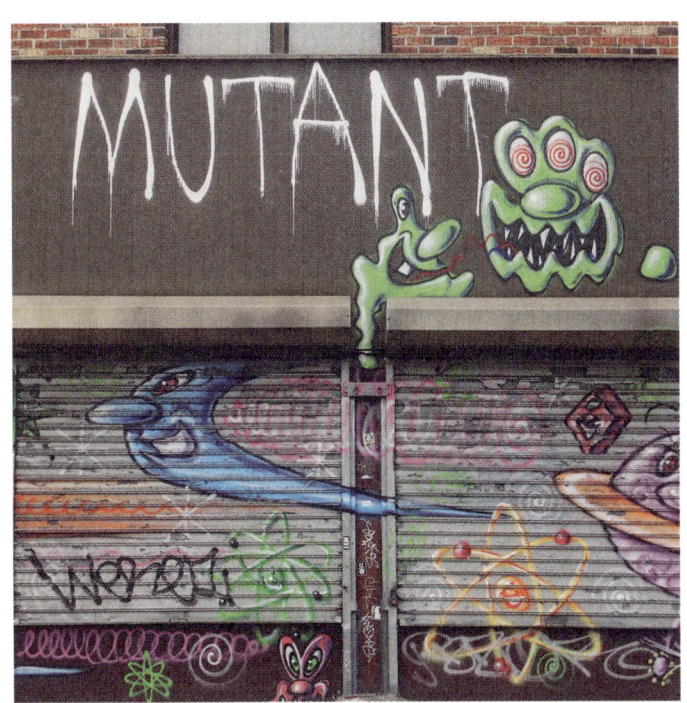
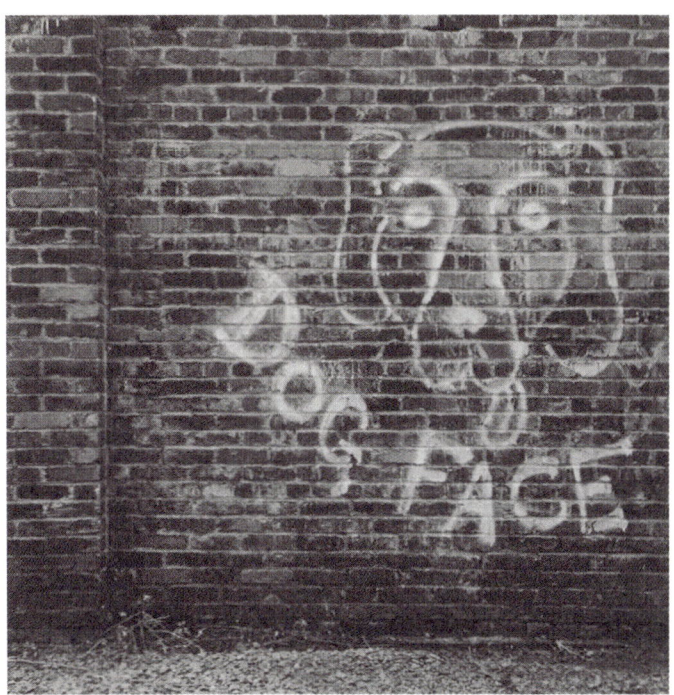

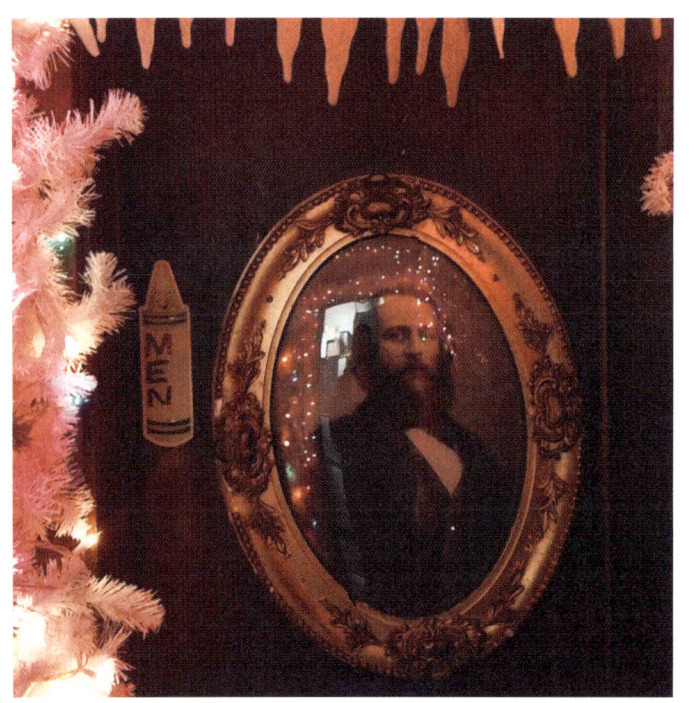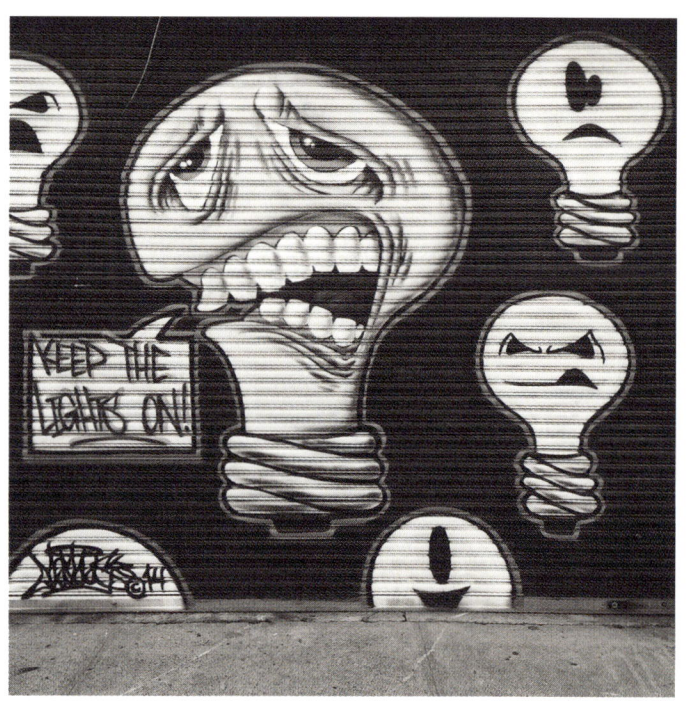

CHAPTER ONE

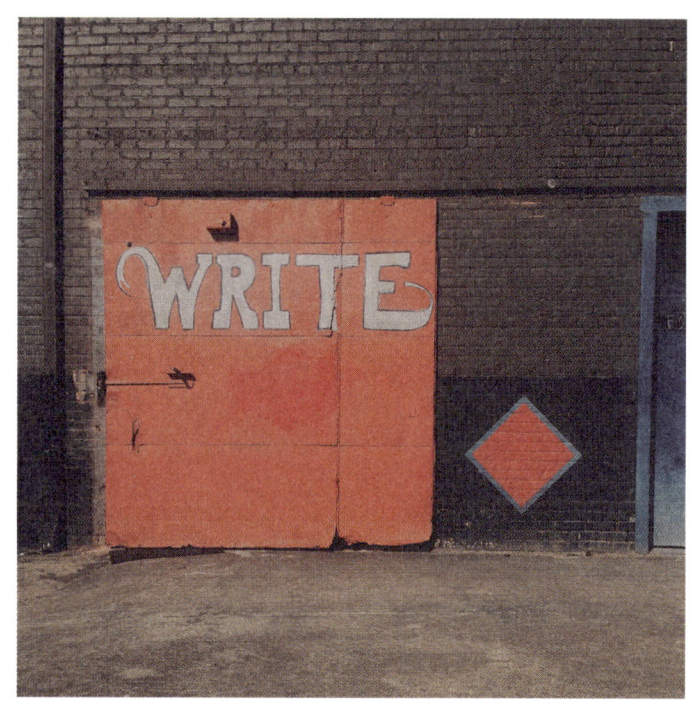

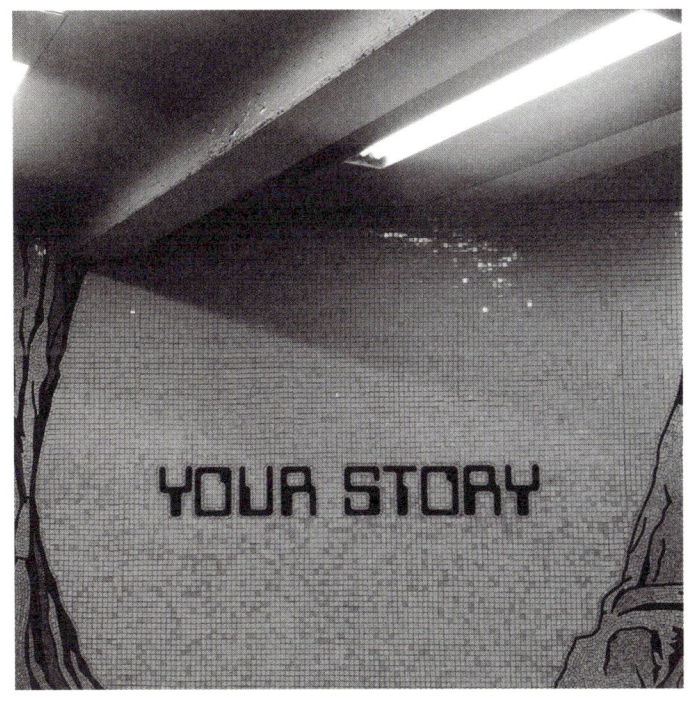

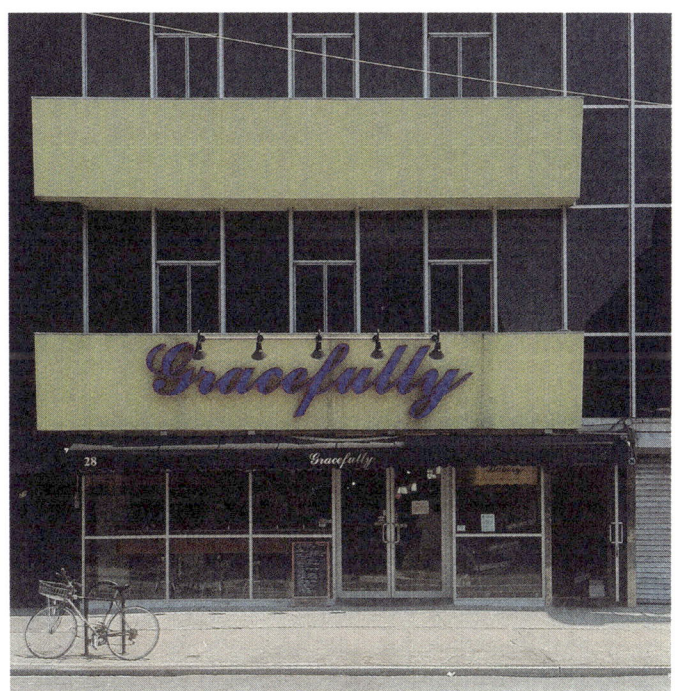

FREAK SHOW

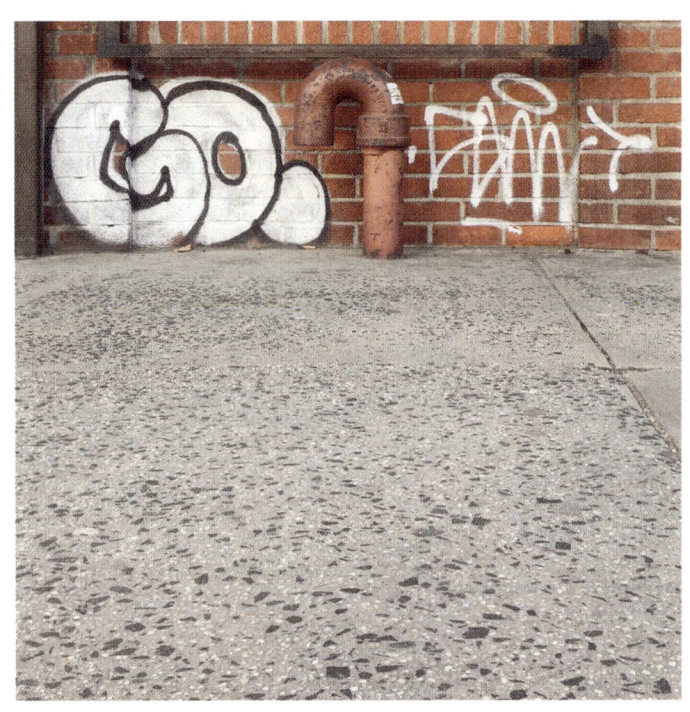

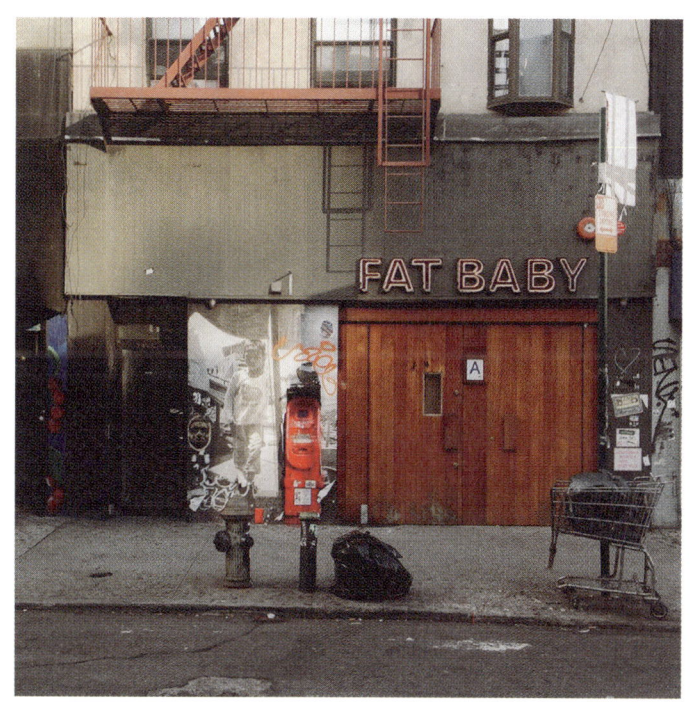
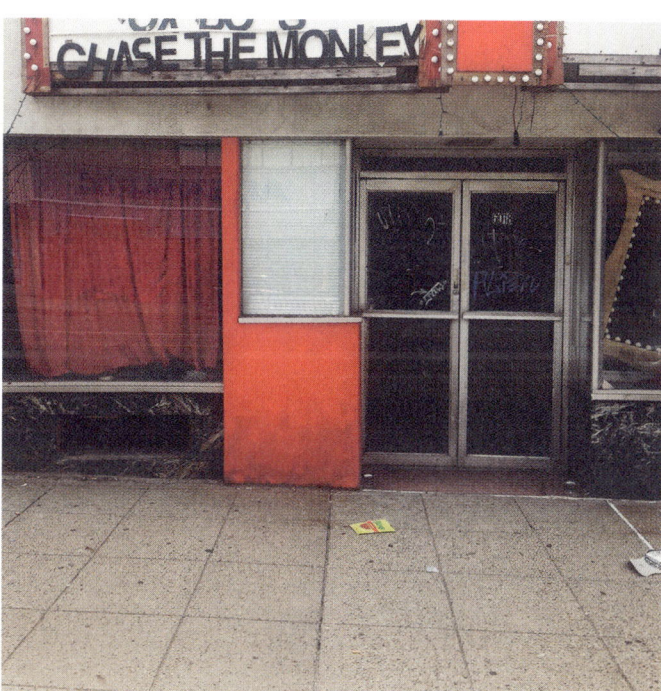

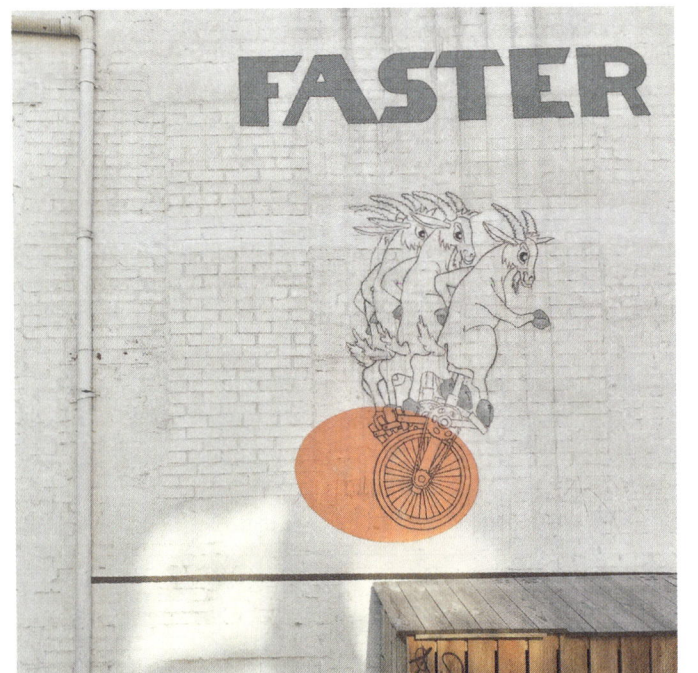
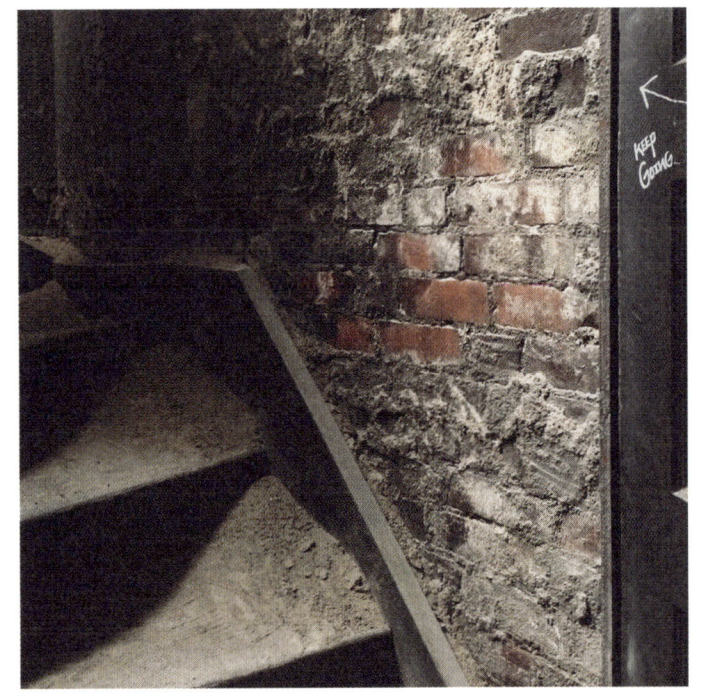

THE DRUNK JOCKEY

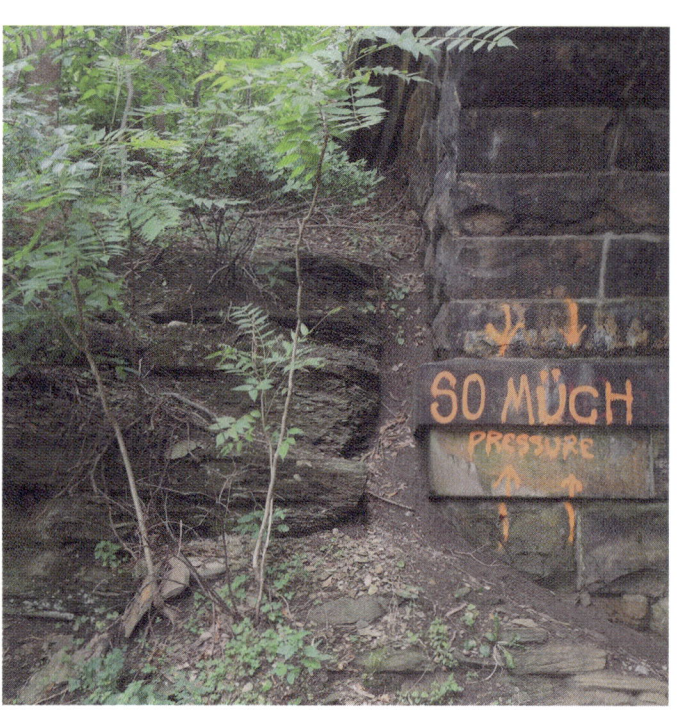

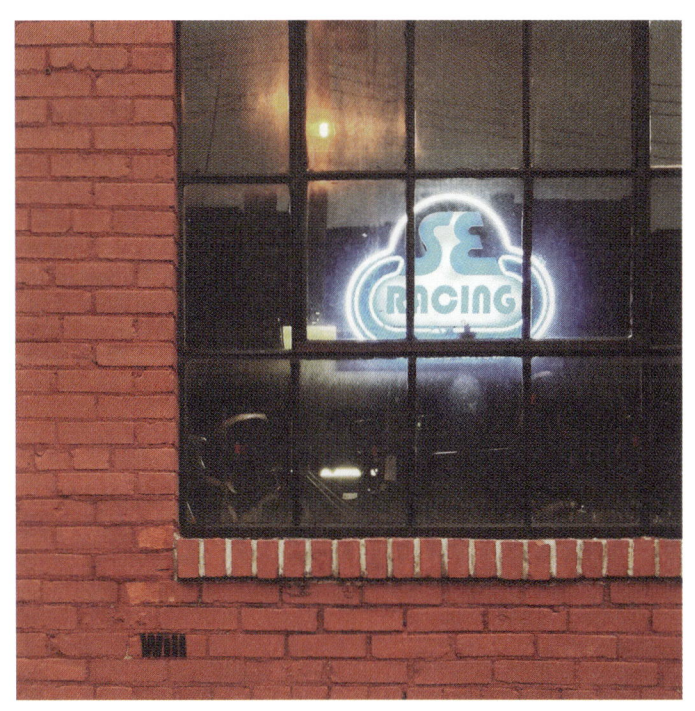
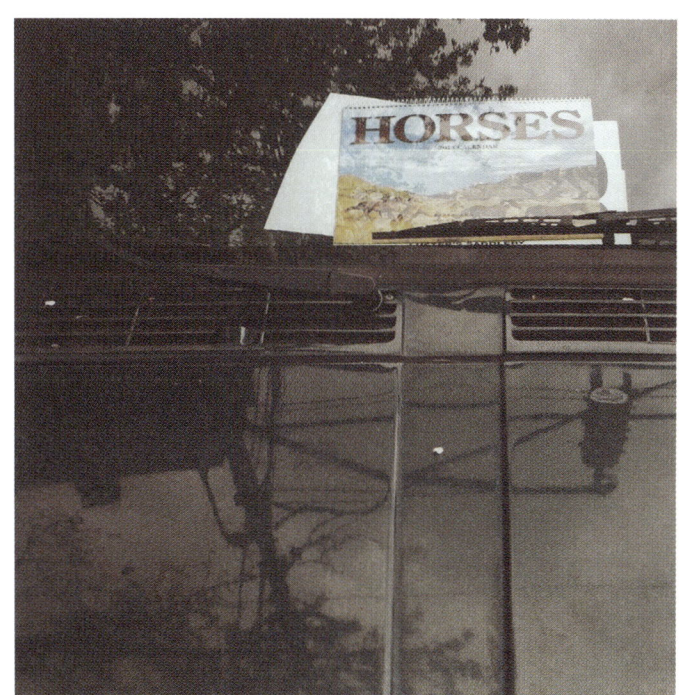

REVELATION

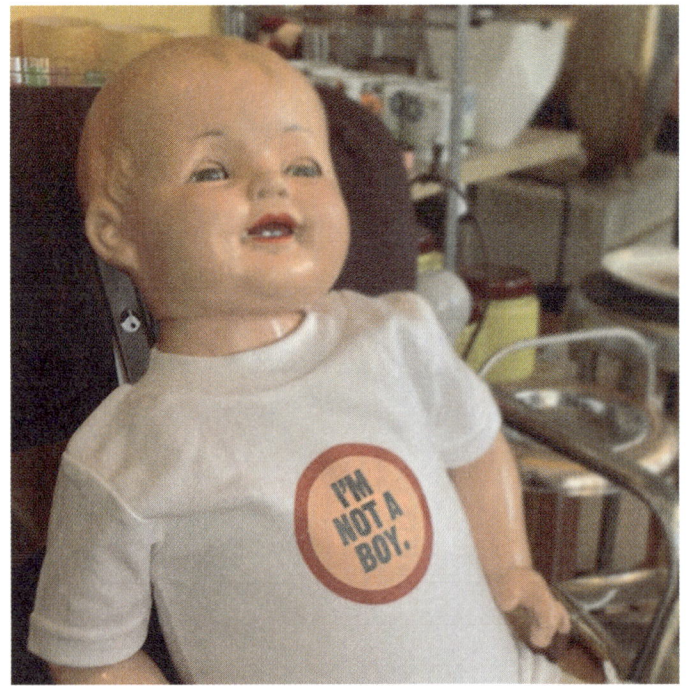

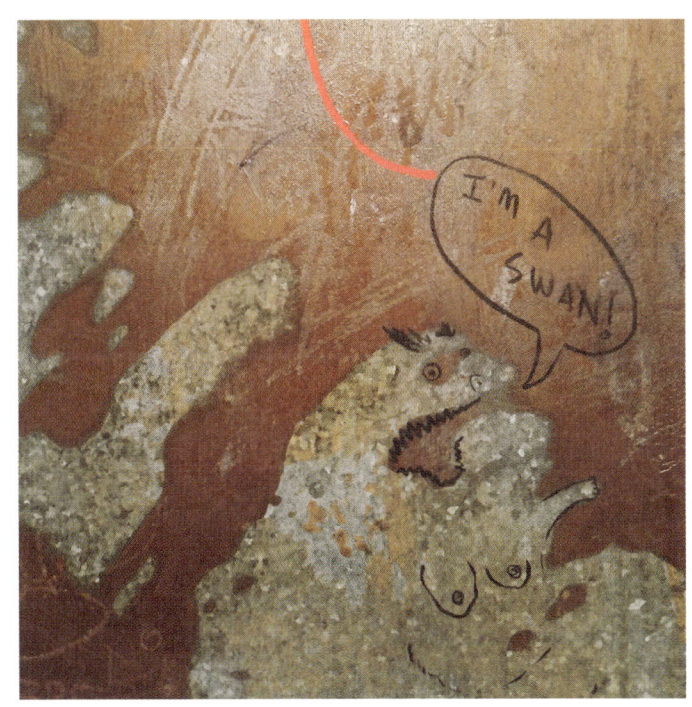

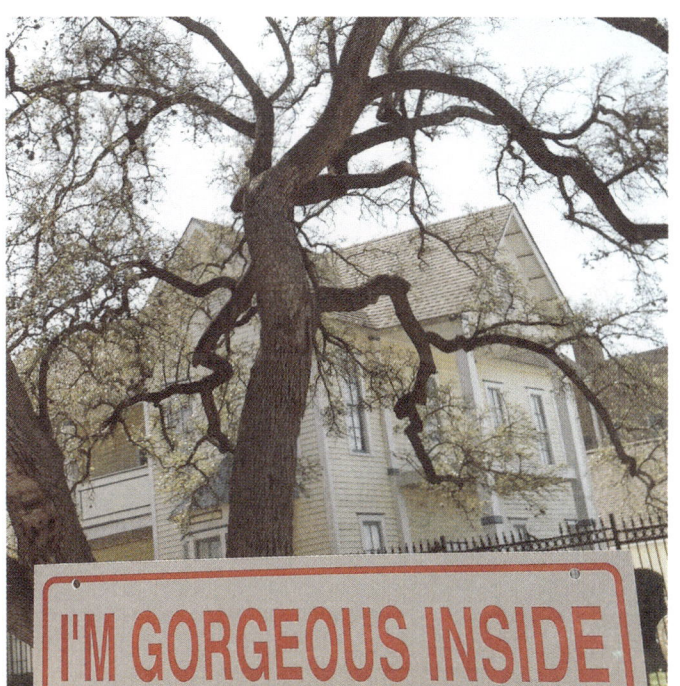

JUST MARRIED

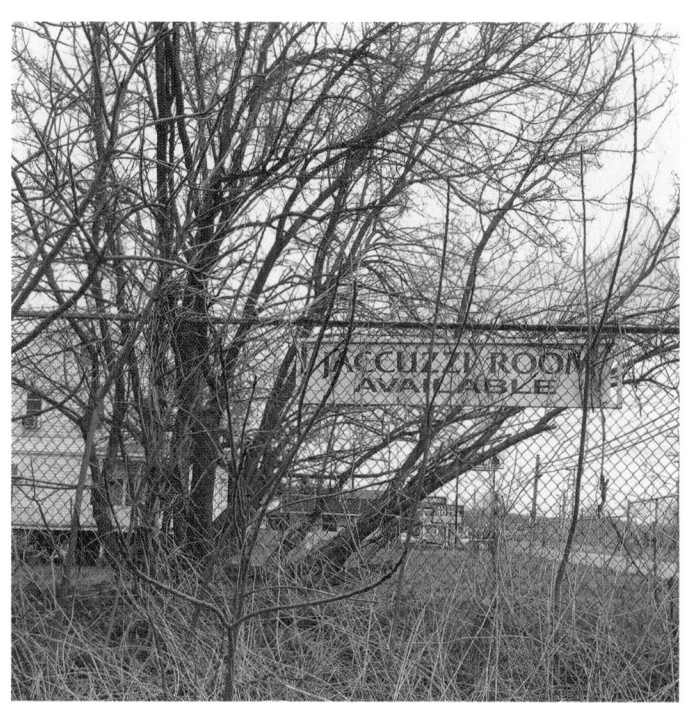

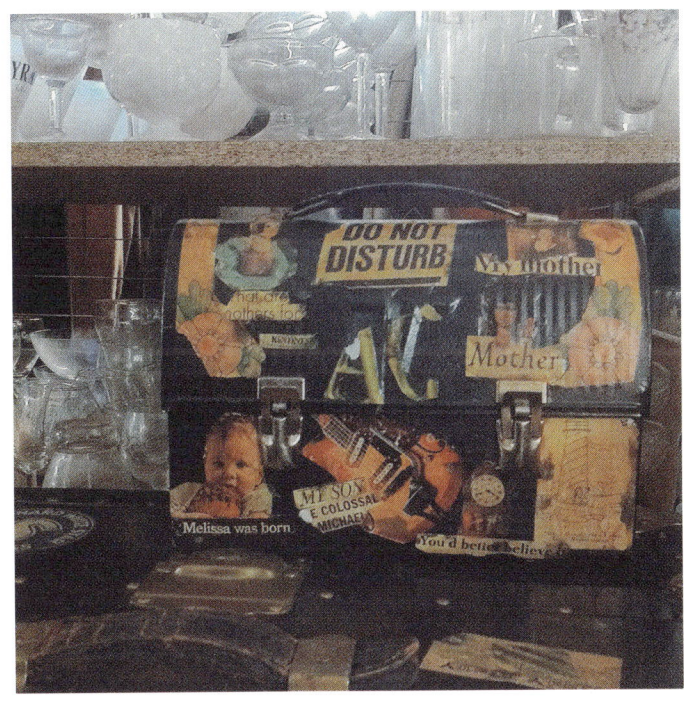

HAND IN HAND

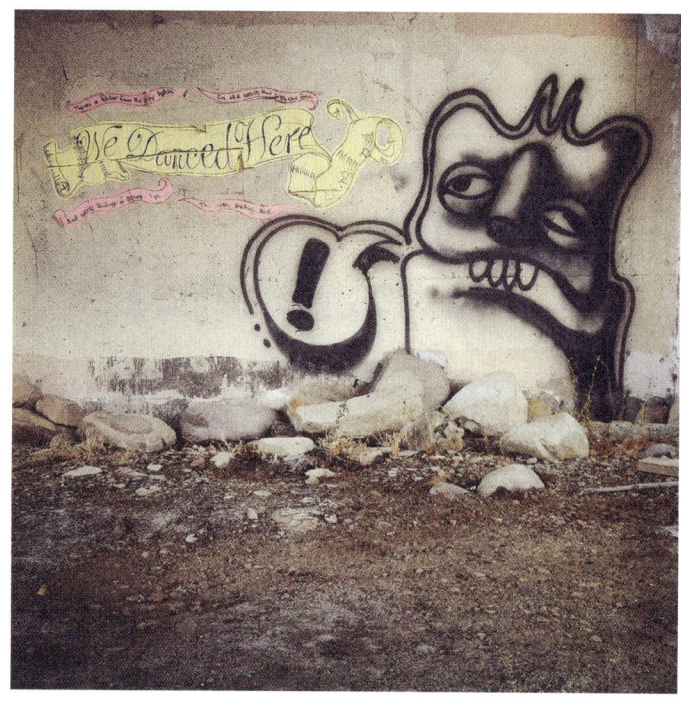

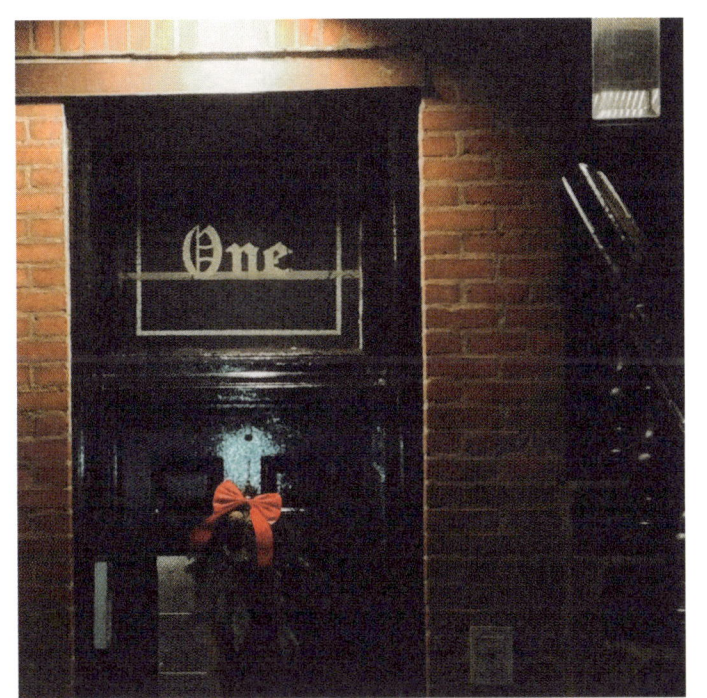
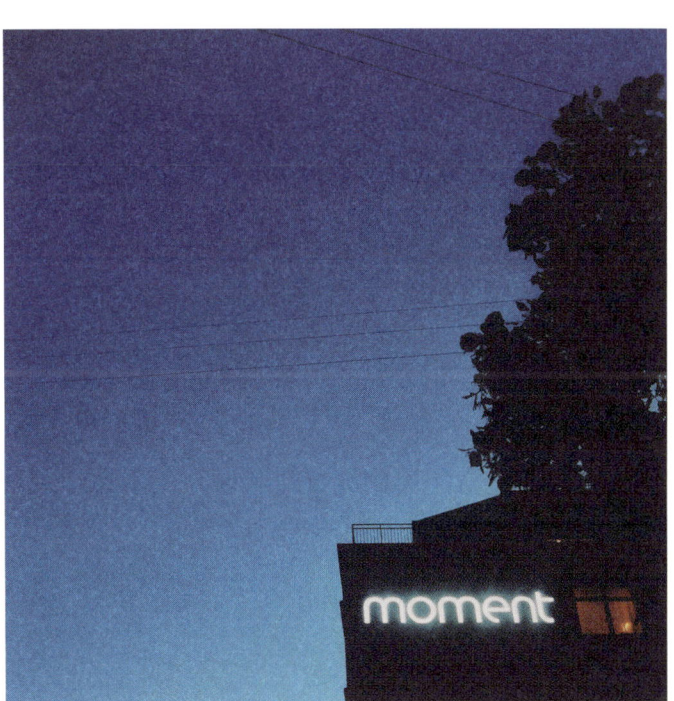

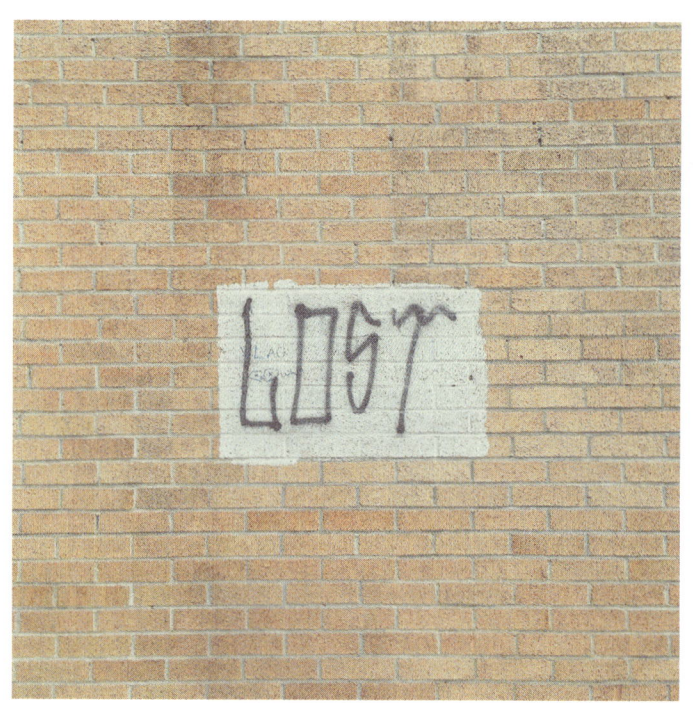

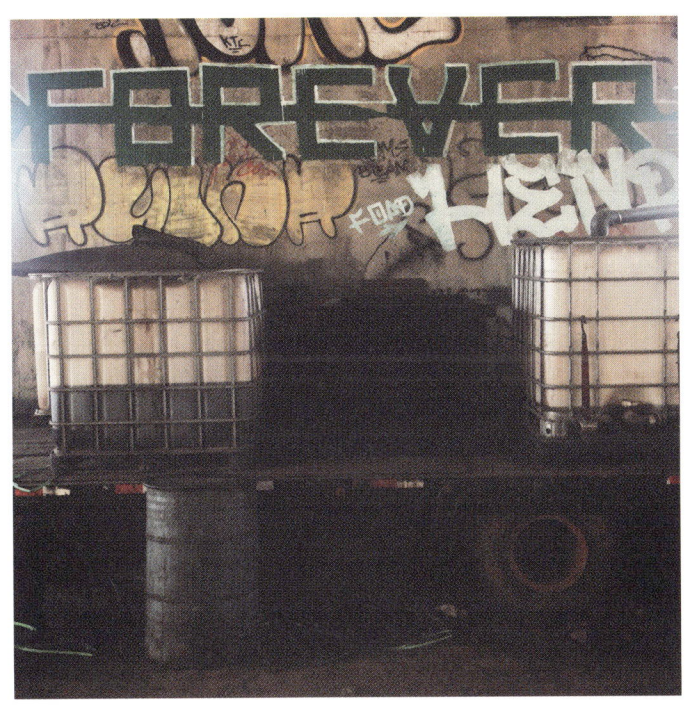

GONE TOO SOON

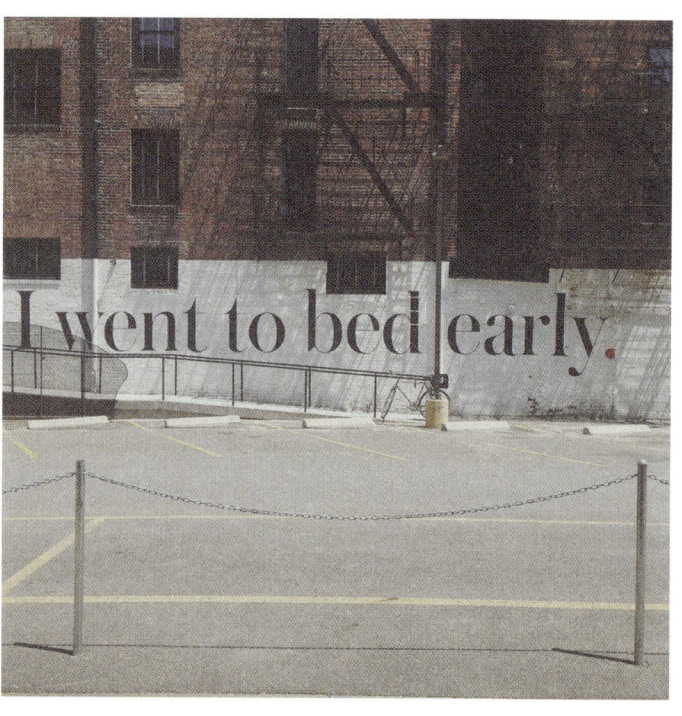

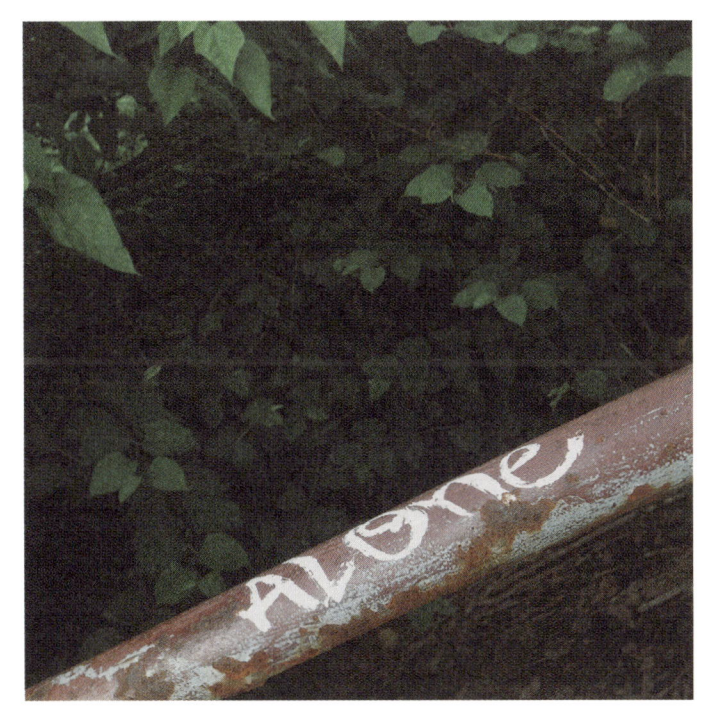
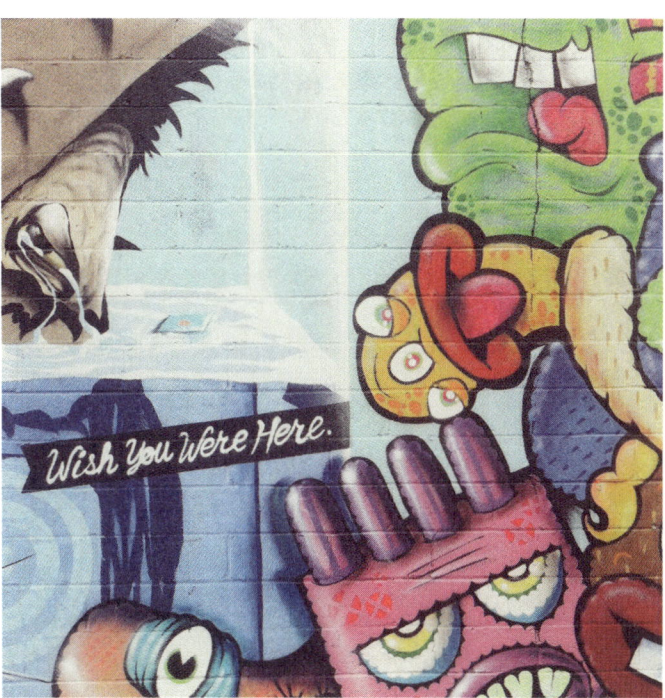

OLD & SENILE

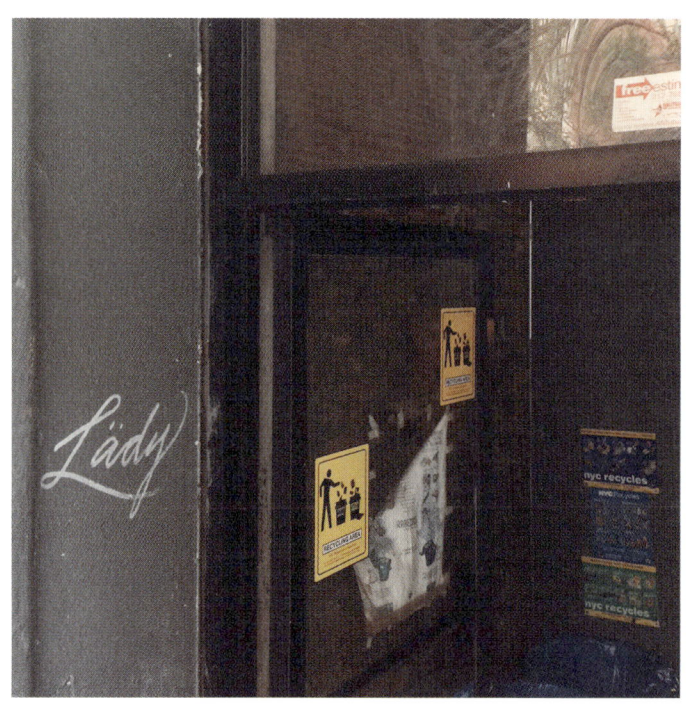

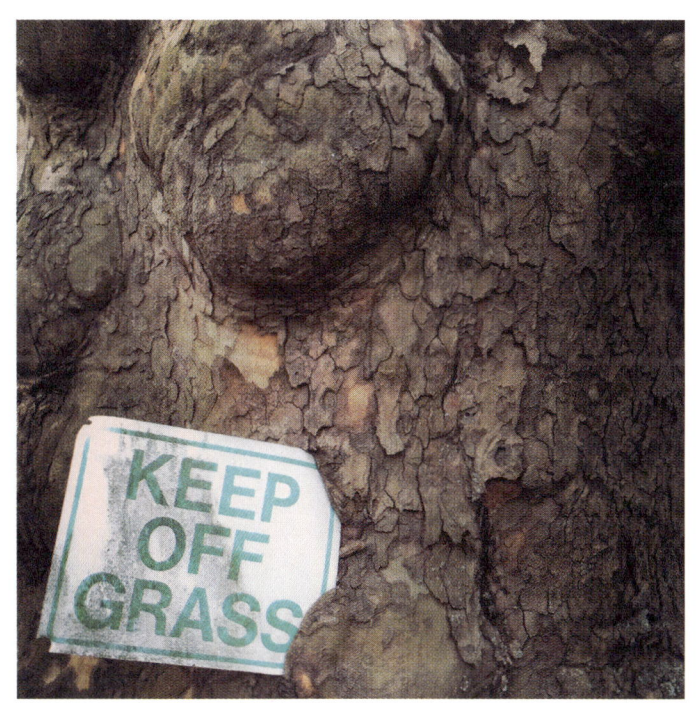
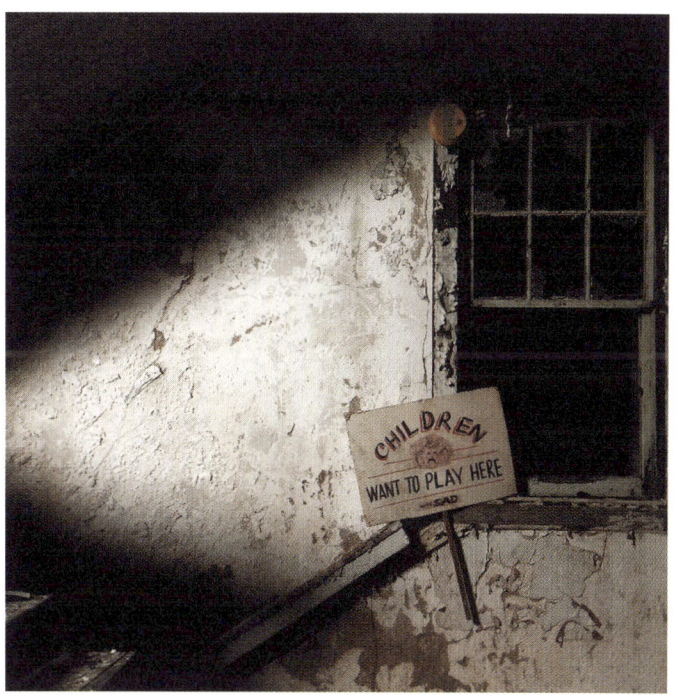

FLIPPER FLIPPED OUT

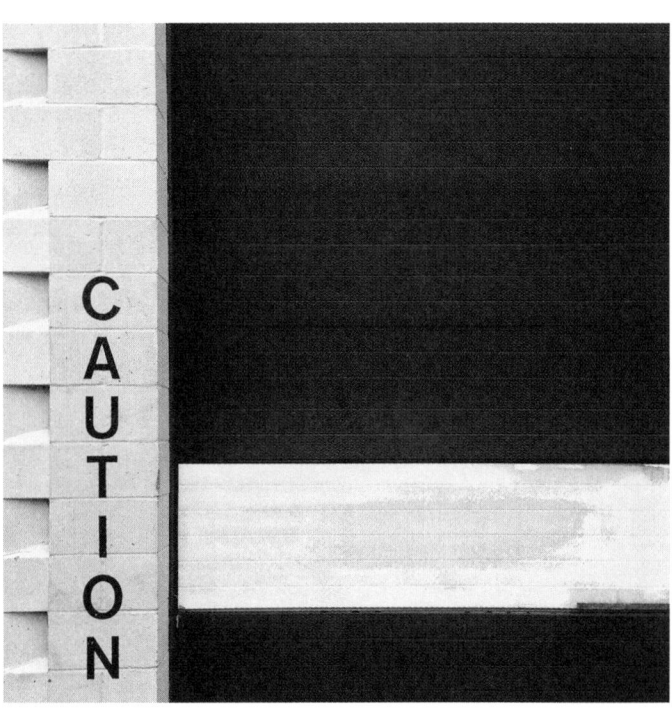

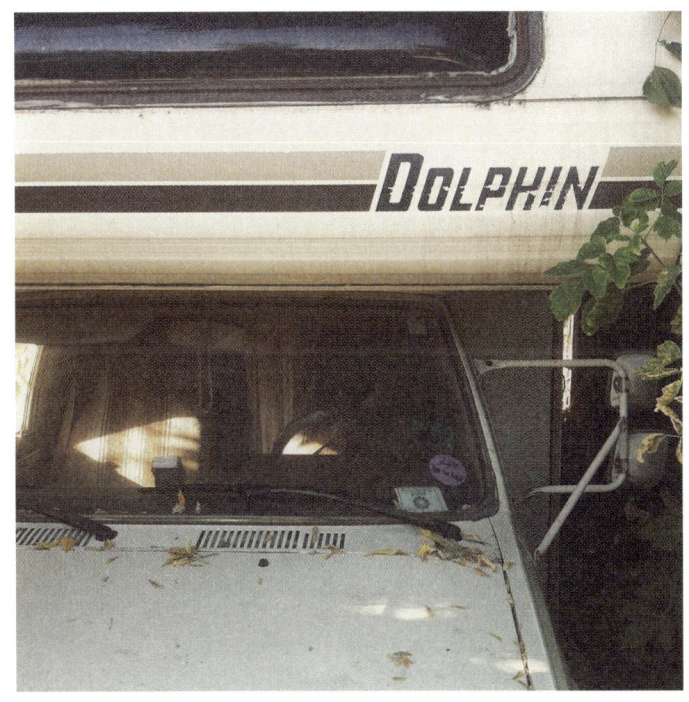

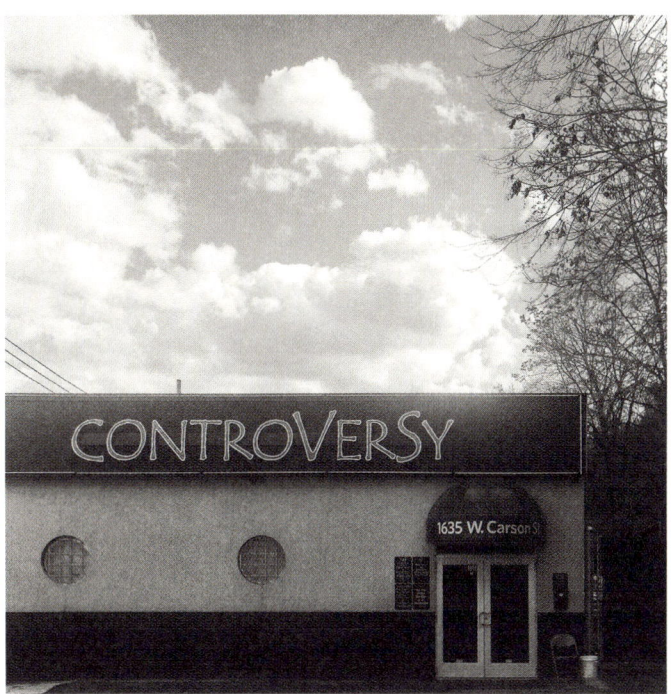

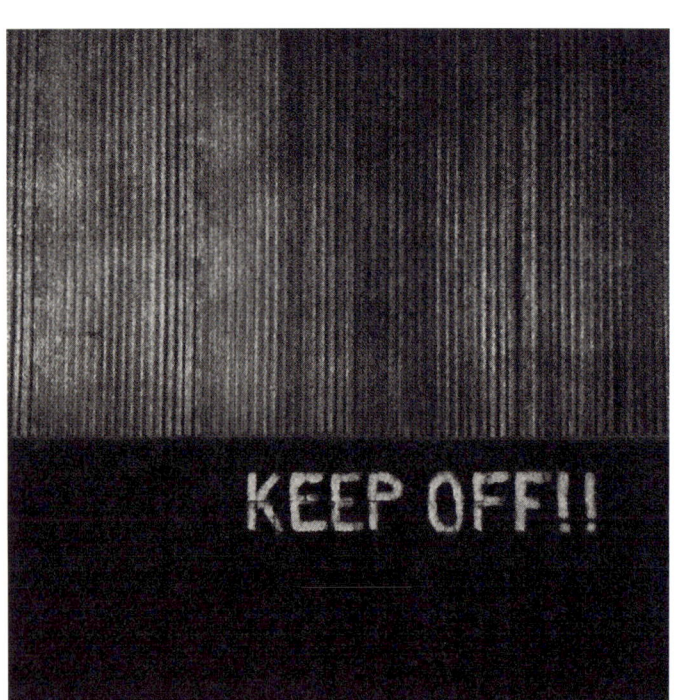

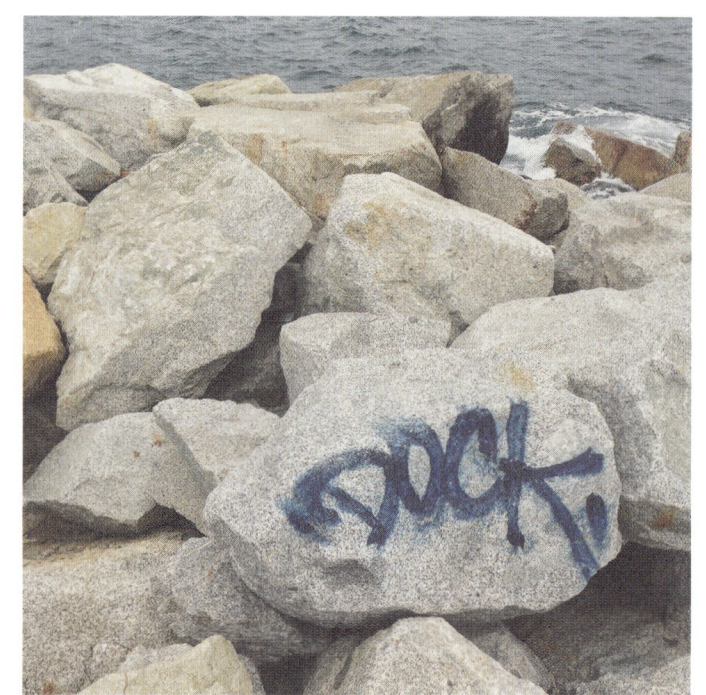

PIT STOP

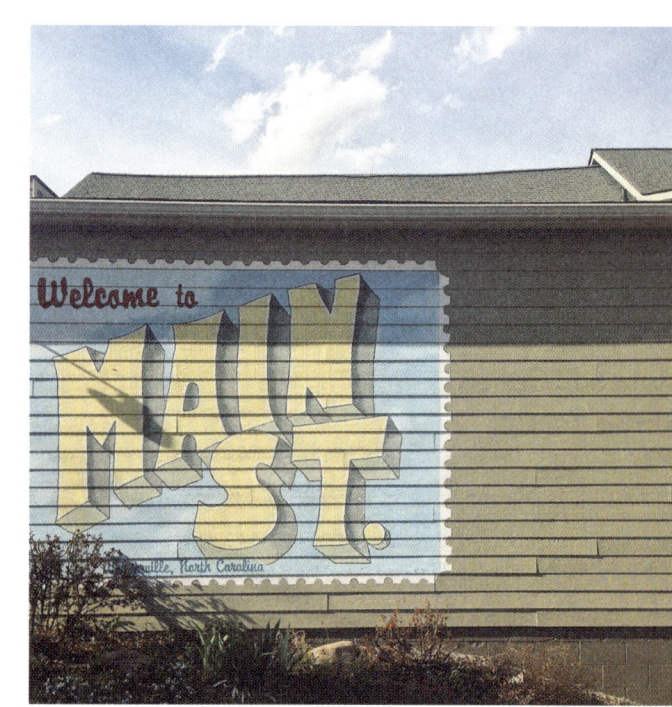

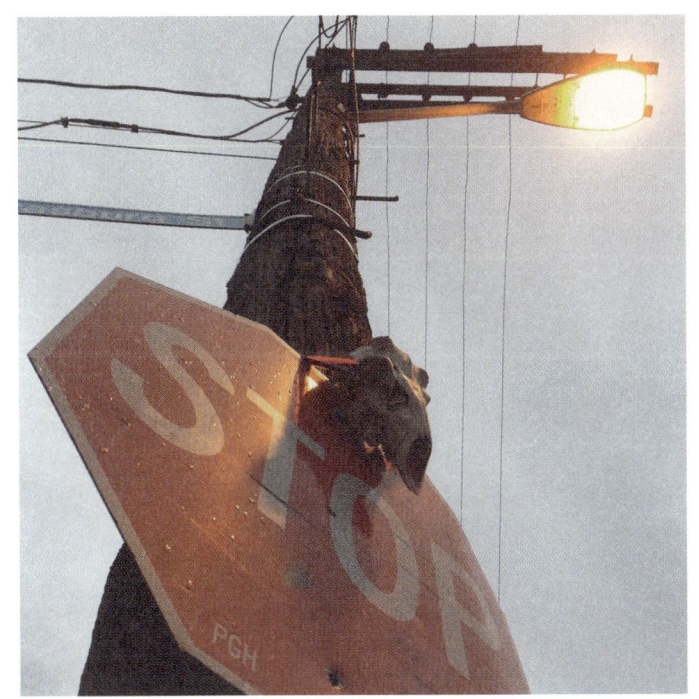
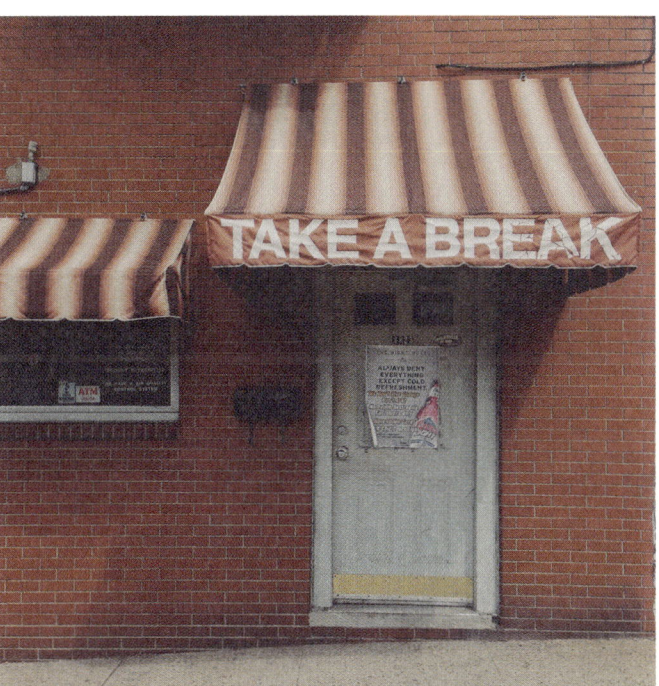

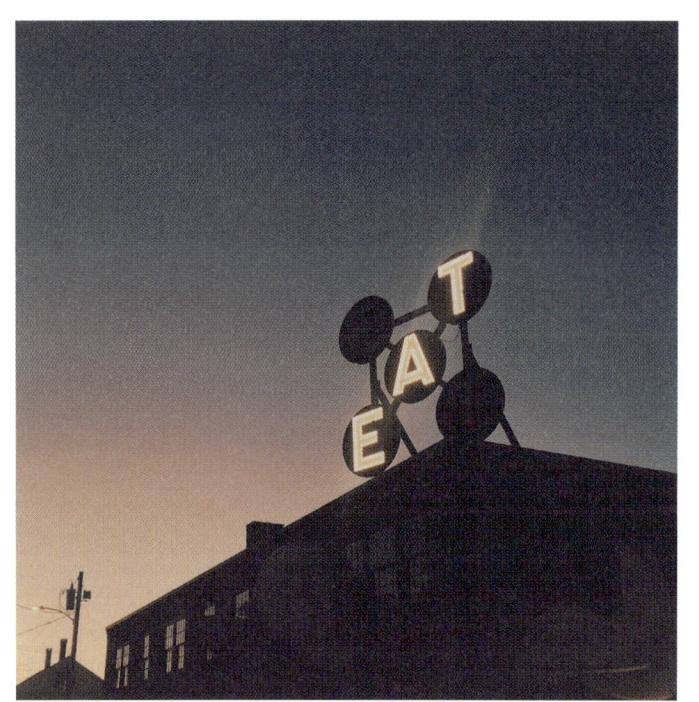
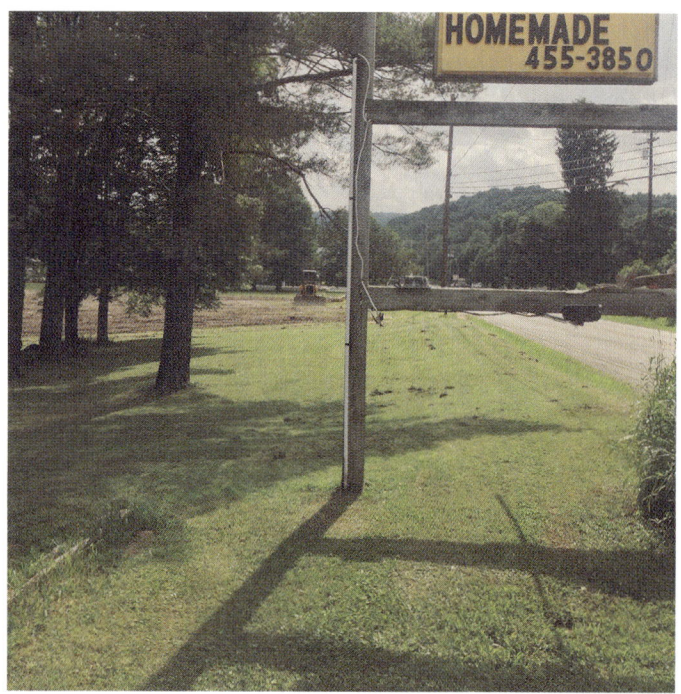

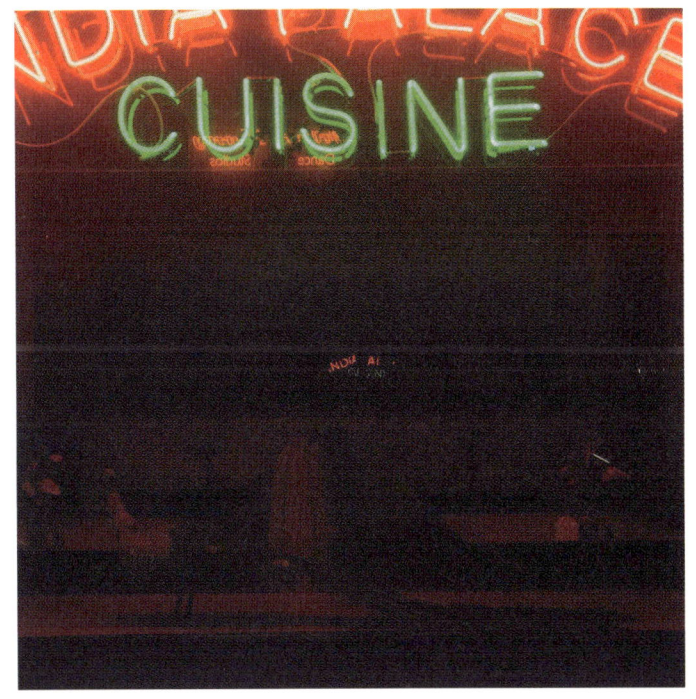
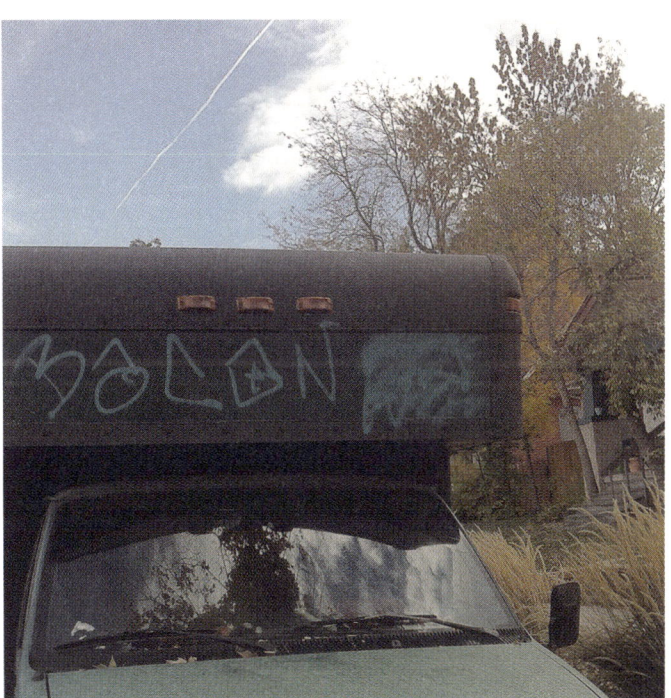

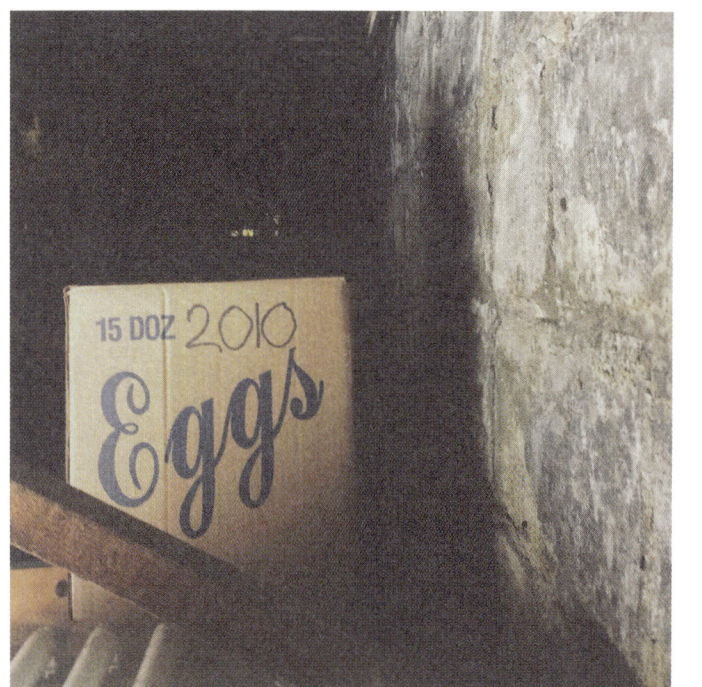
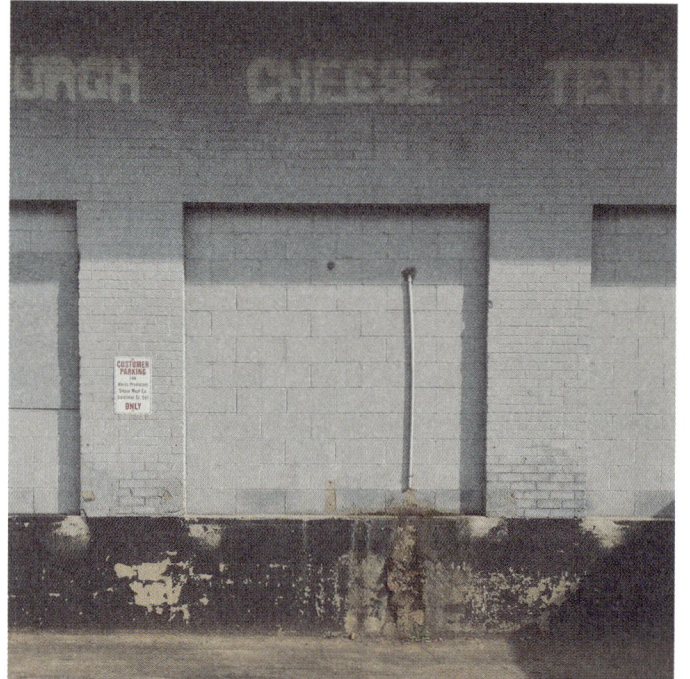

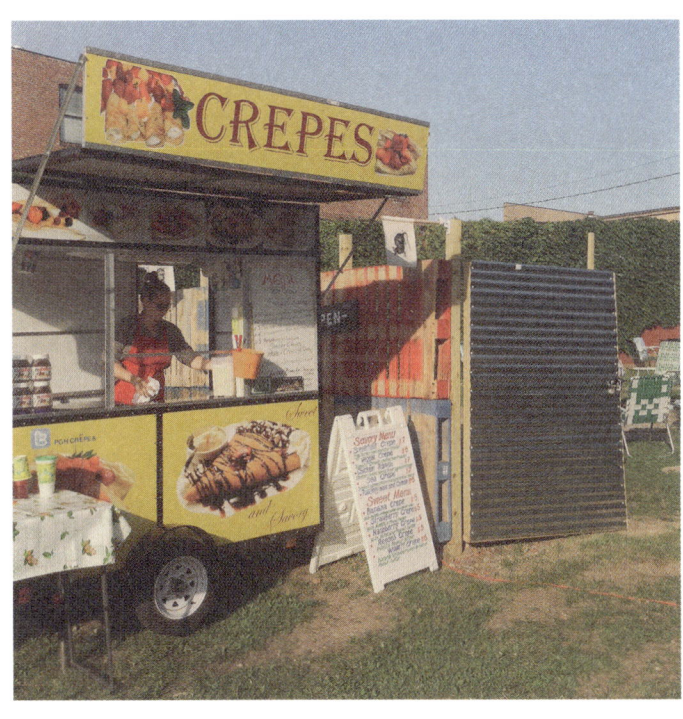

A REQUEST

FROM THE QUEEN

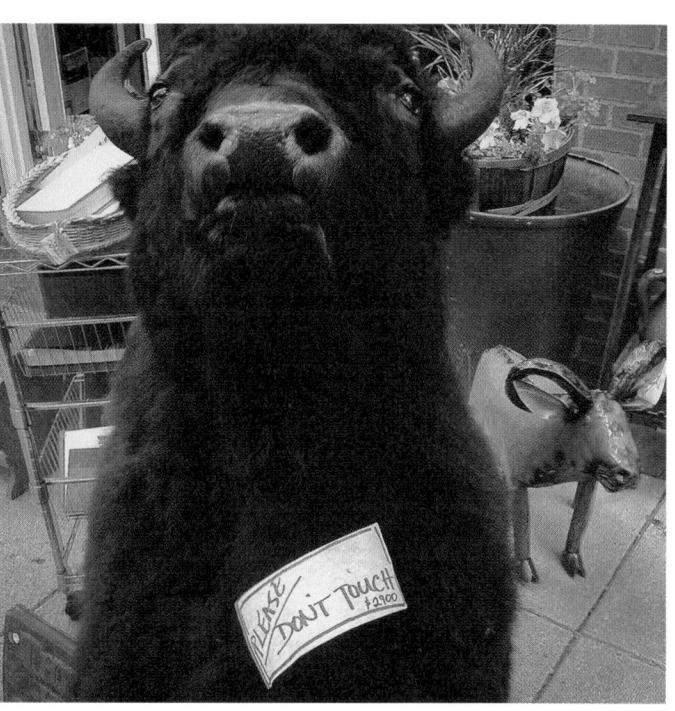

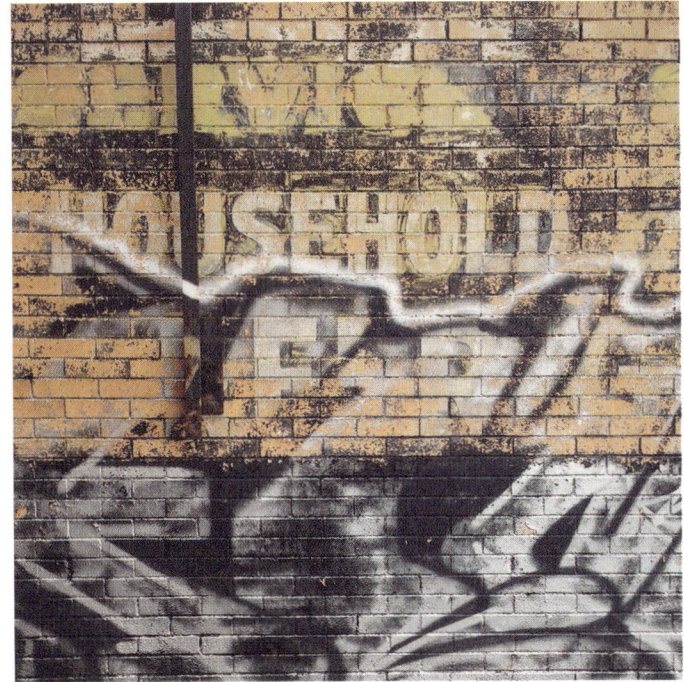
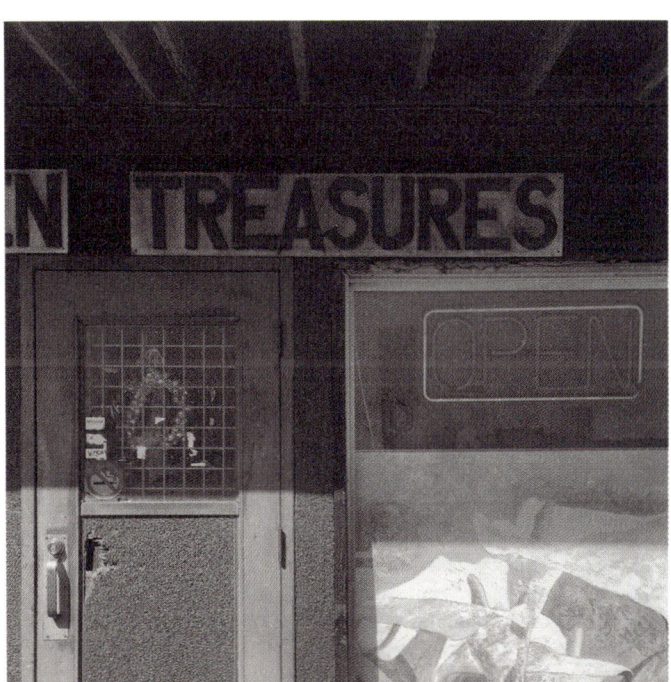

LAST GOODBYE

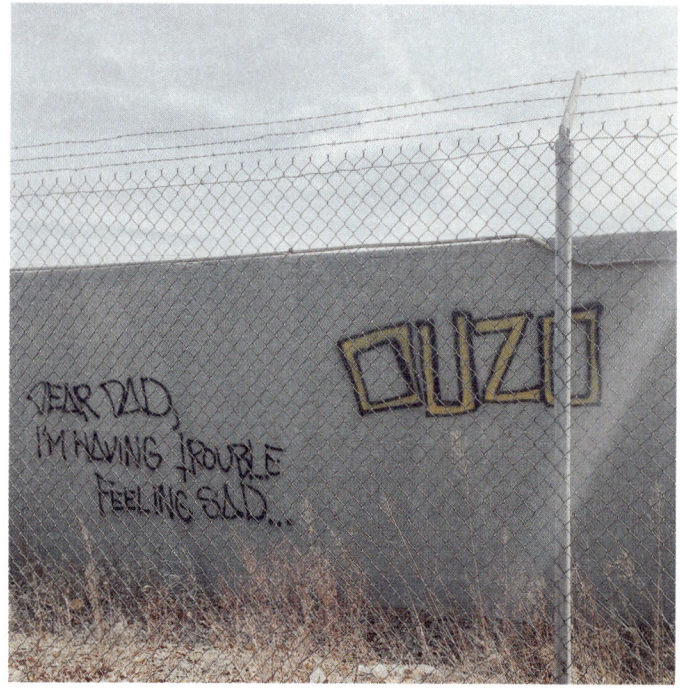

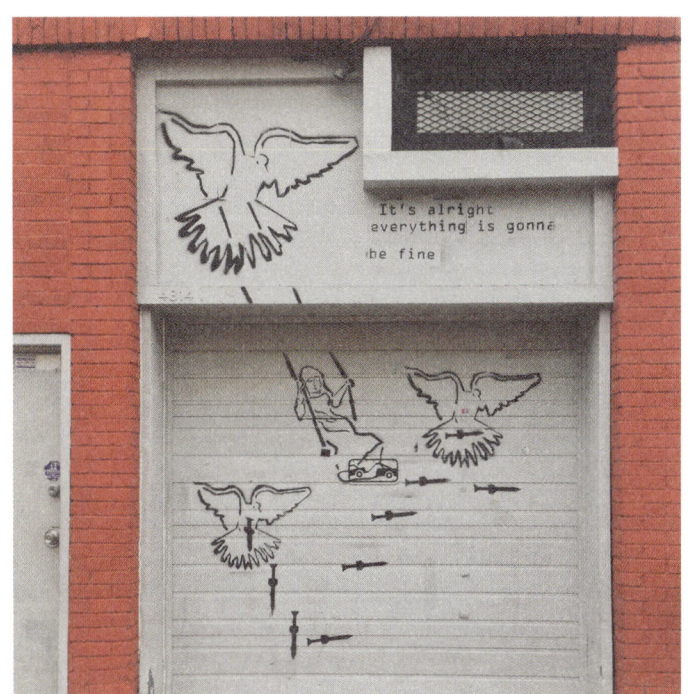

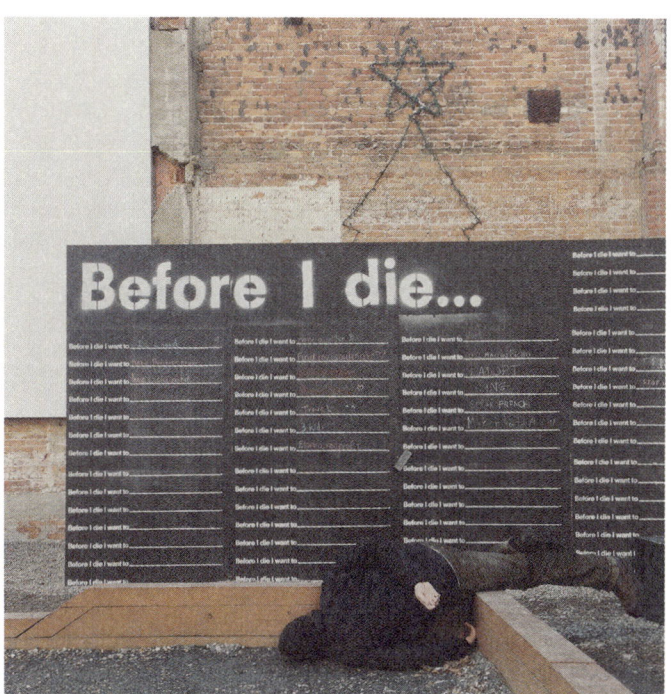

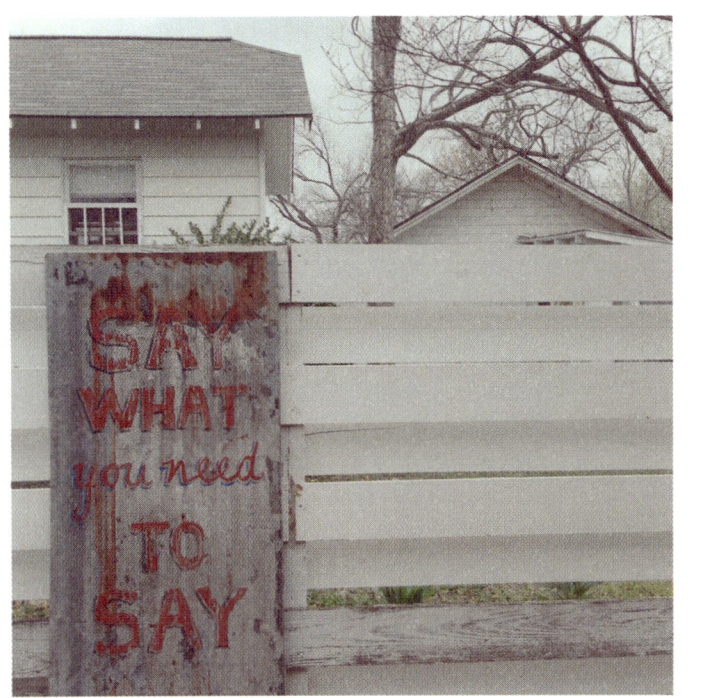
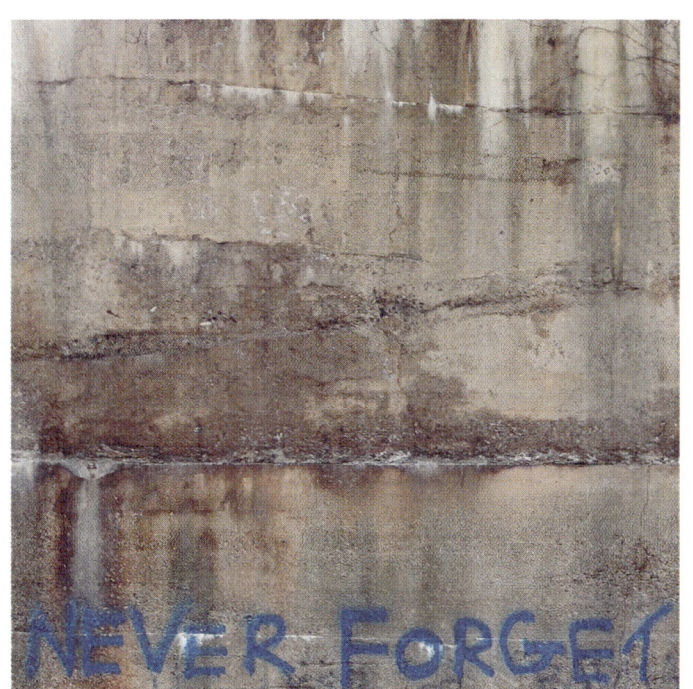

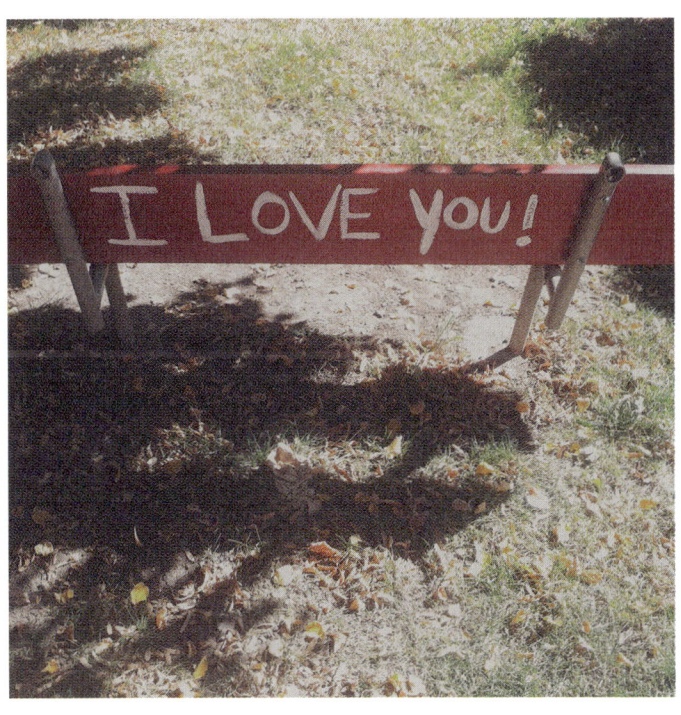

AND THEY'RE

OFF

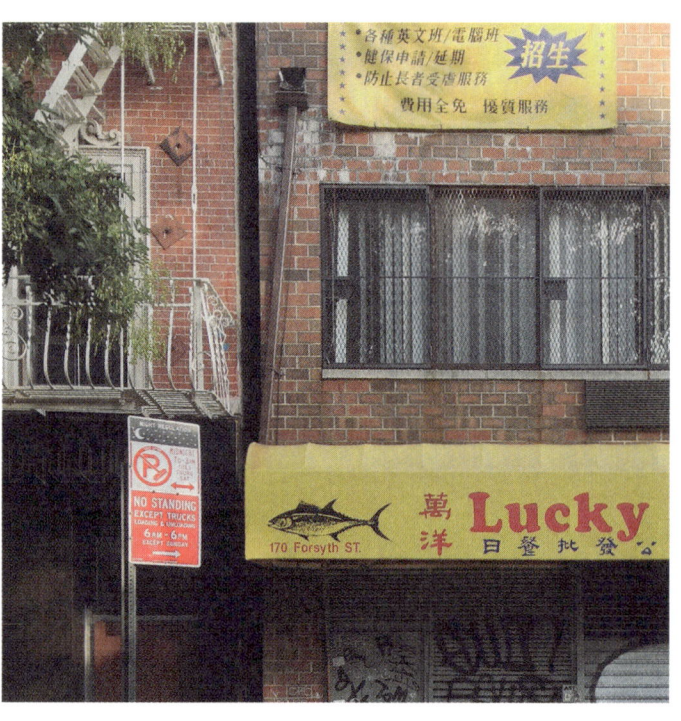

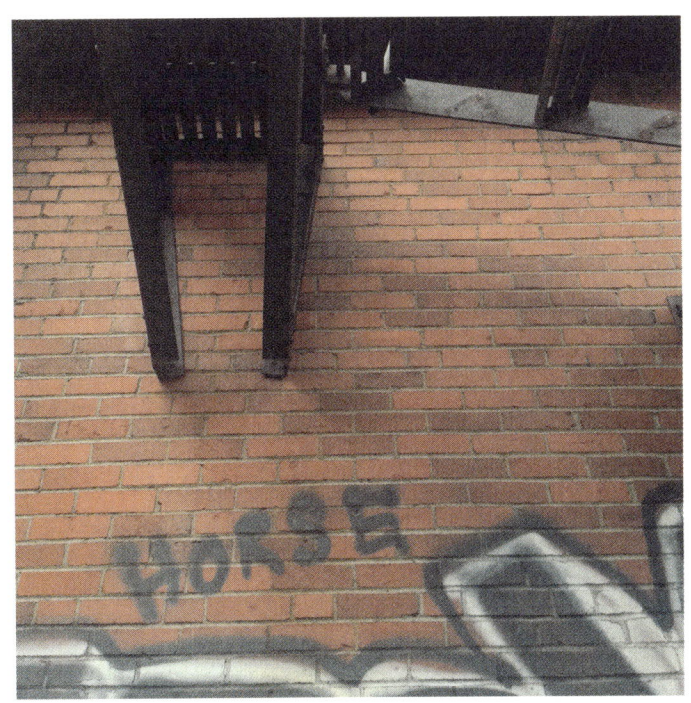
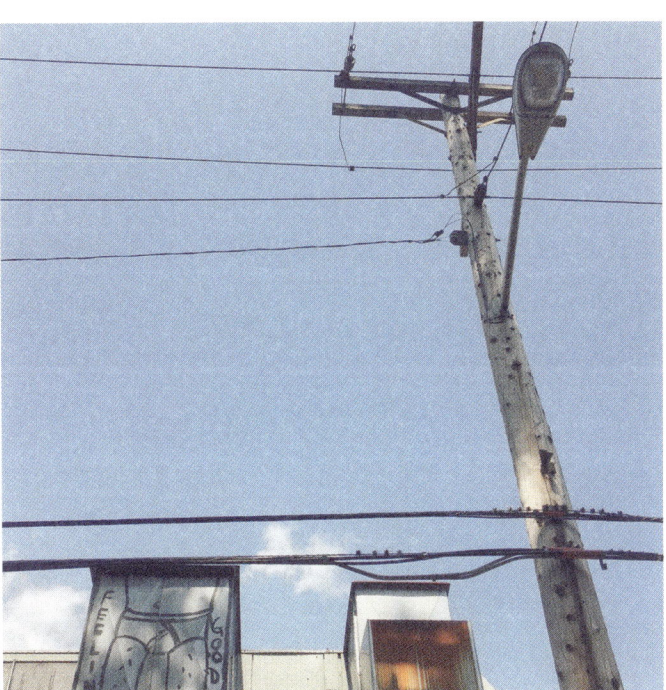

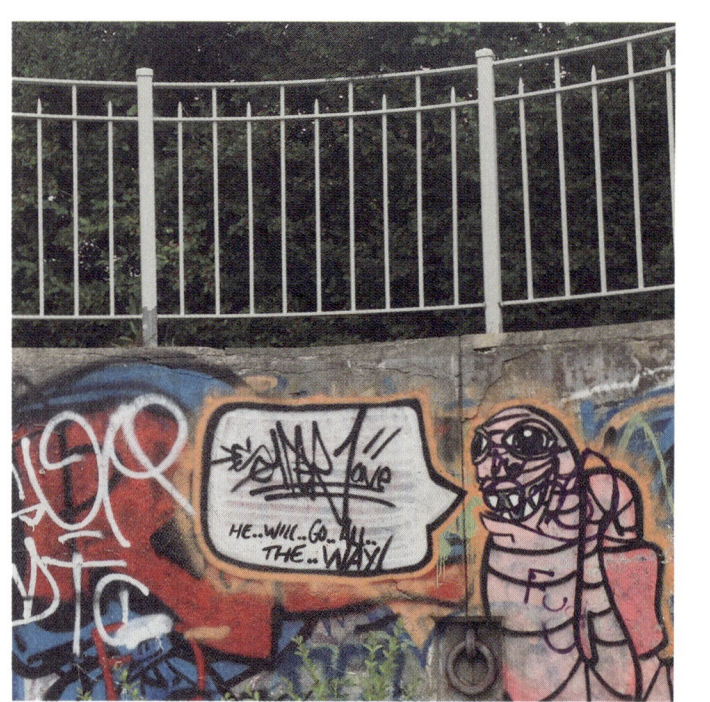
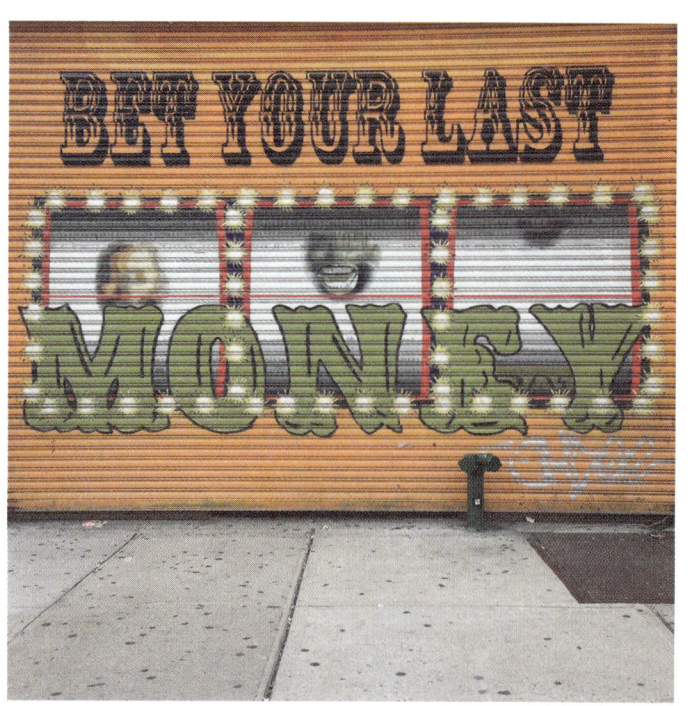

CHEF'S SPECIAL

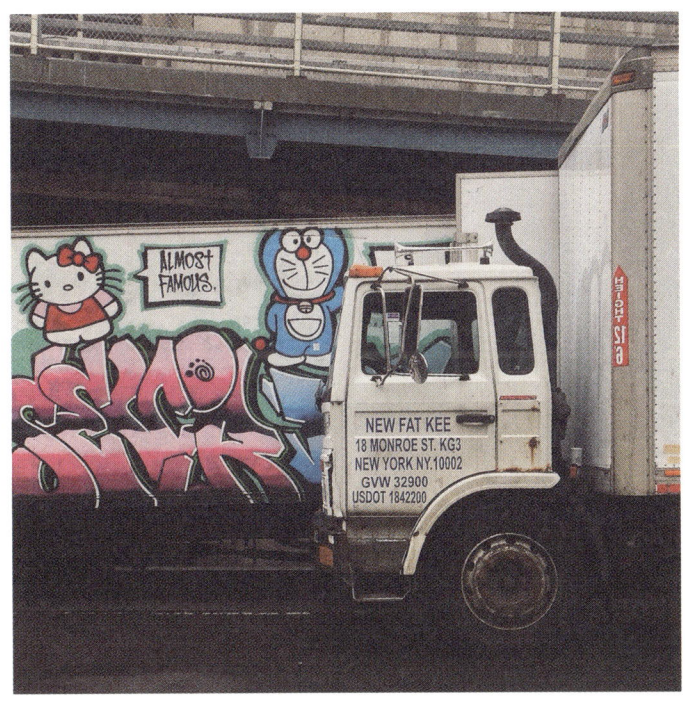

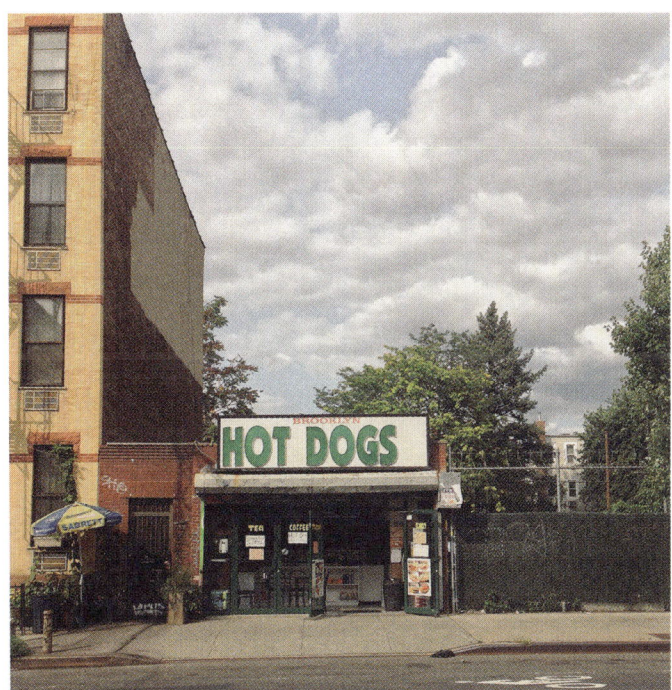

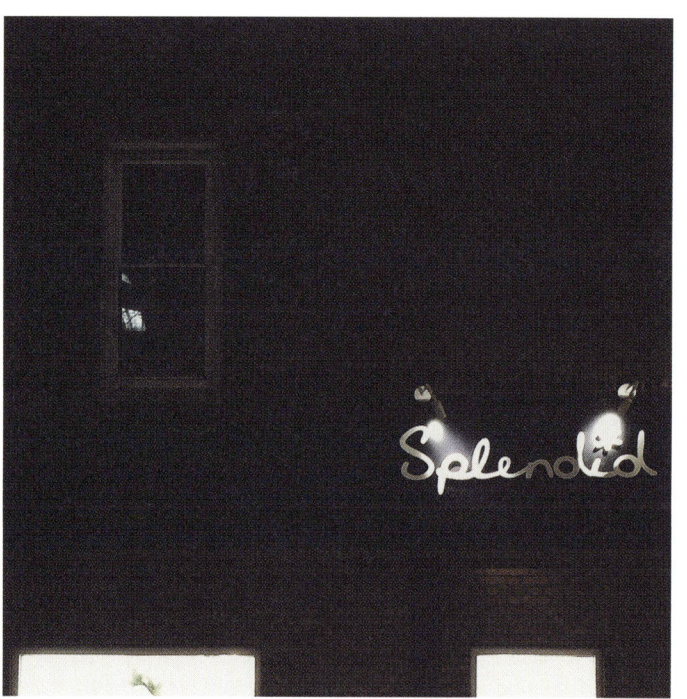

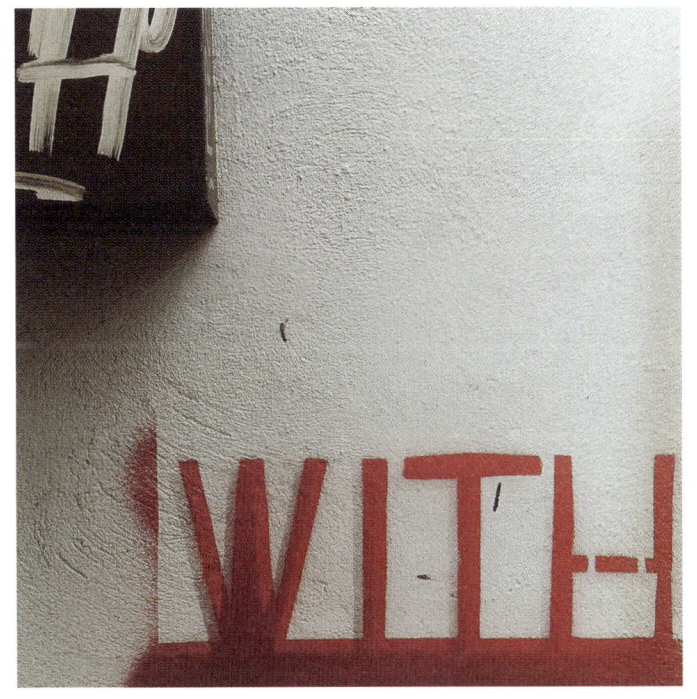
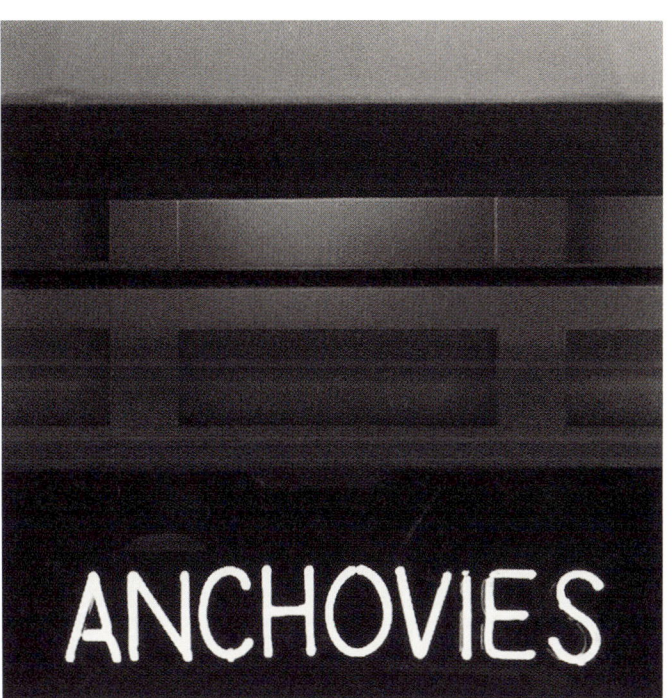

MIND LOST

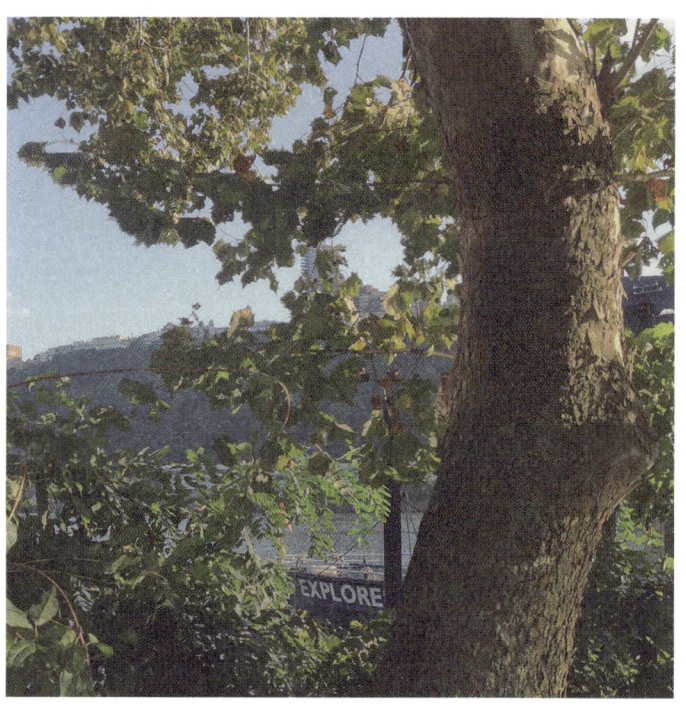

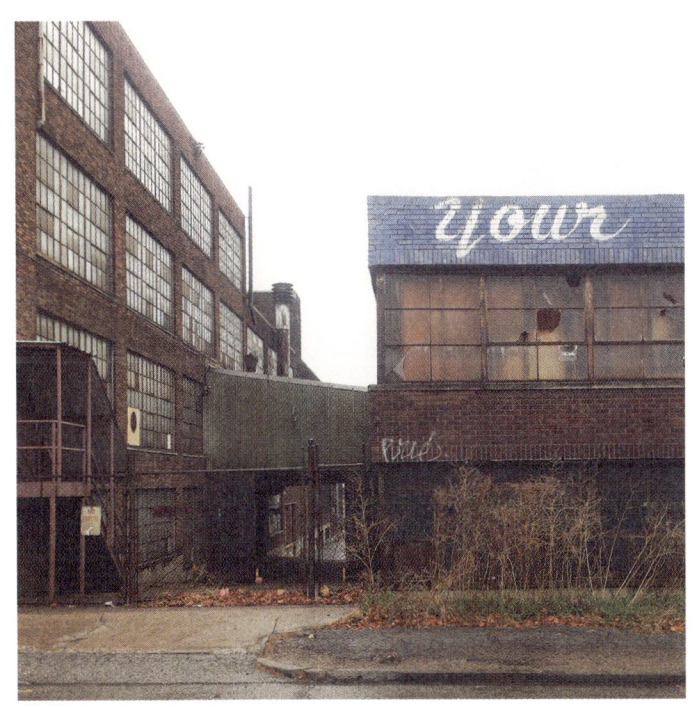

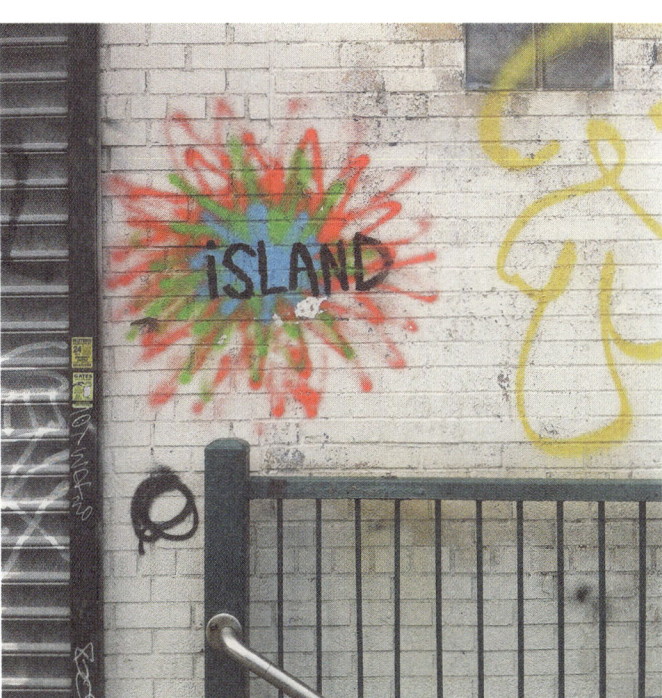

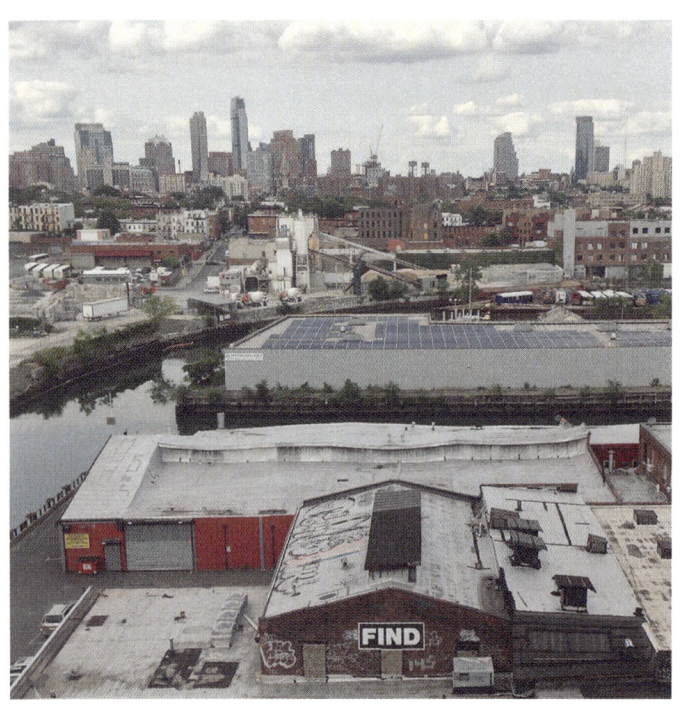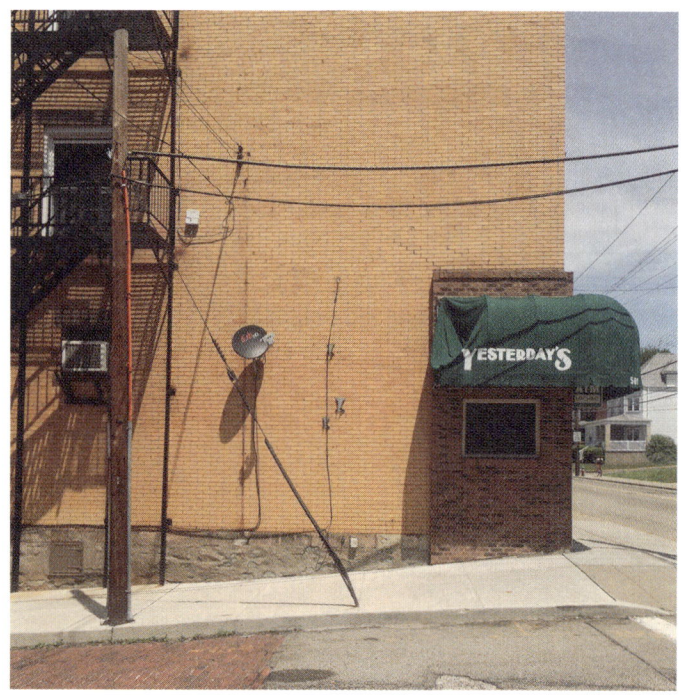

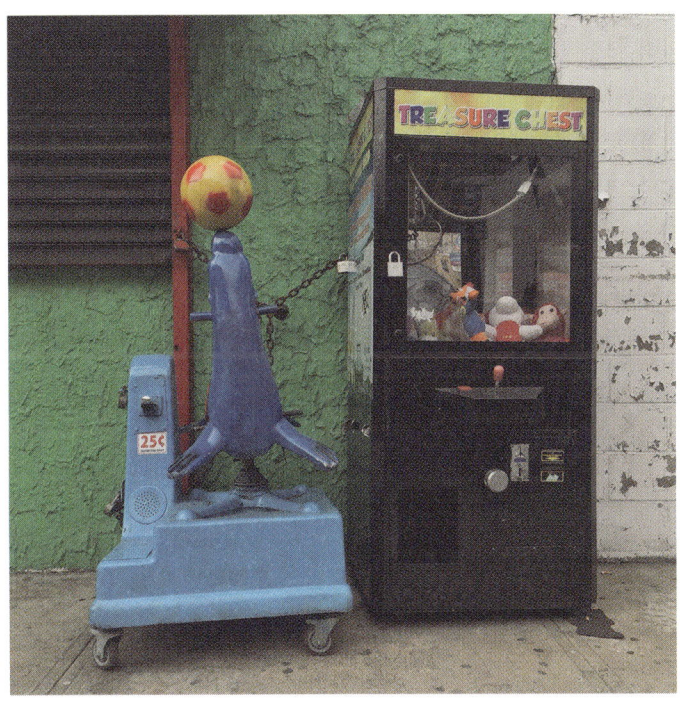

MOTHER'S SECRET

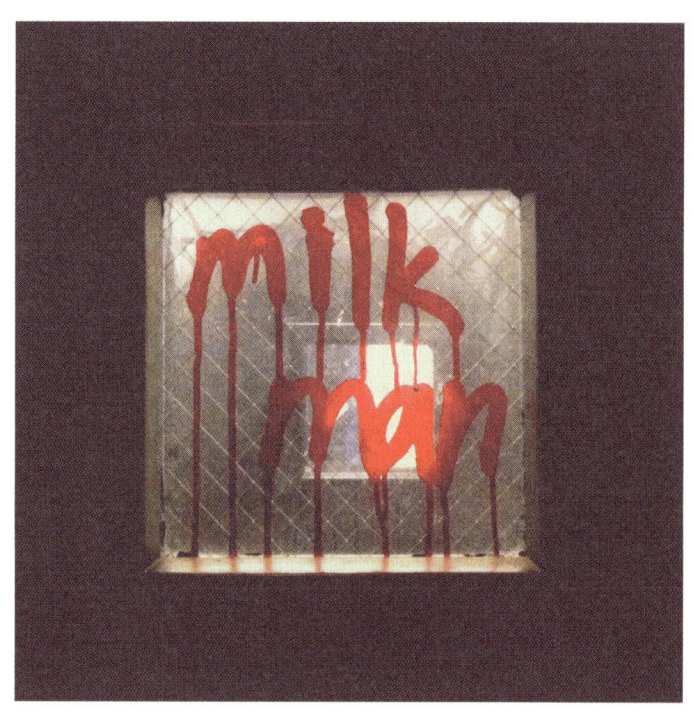

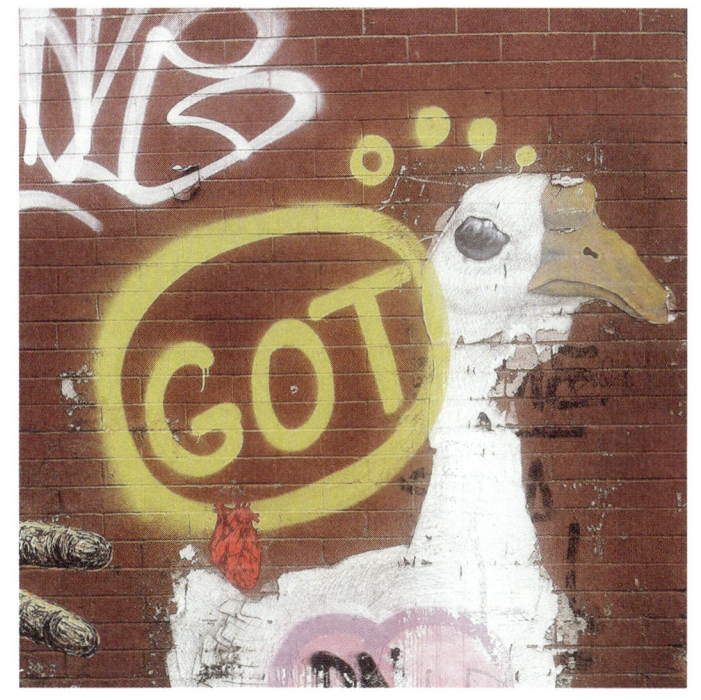
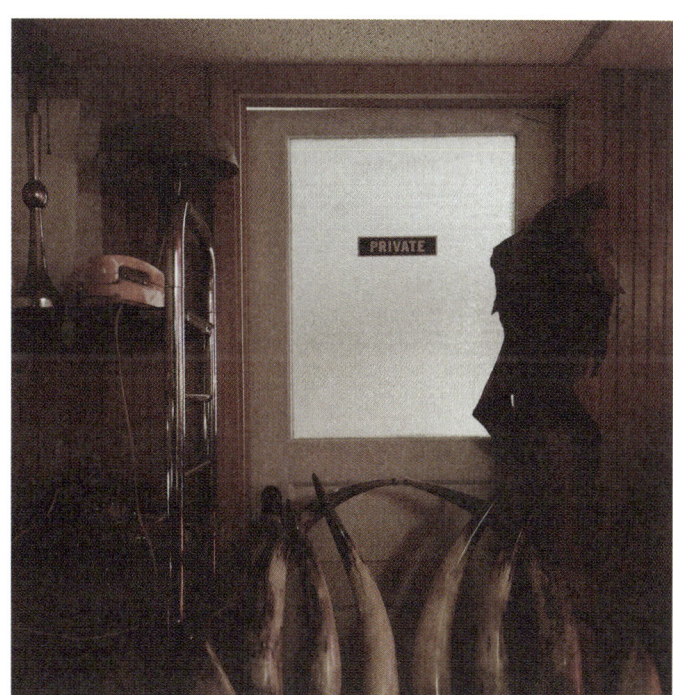

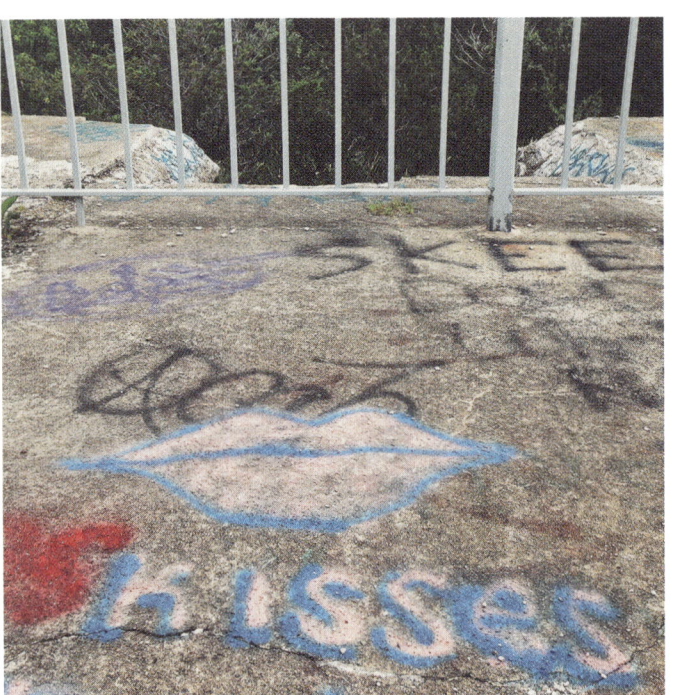
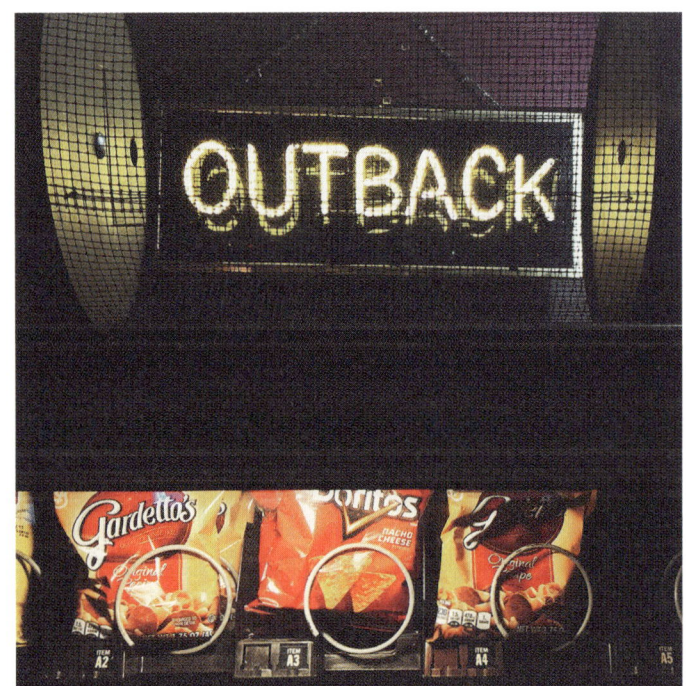

CAGE MATCH

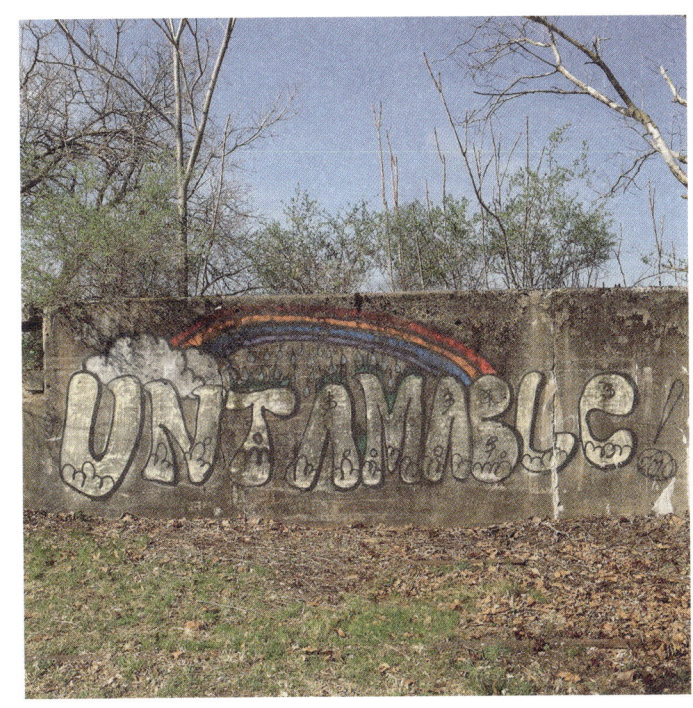

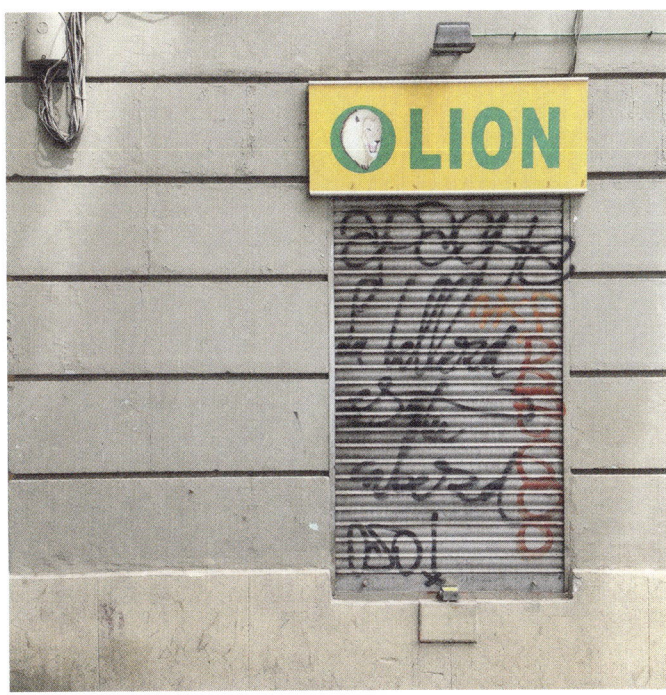

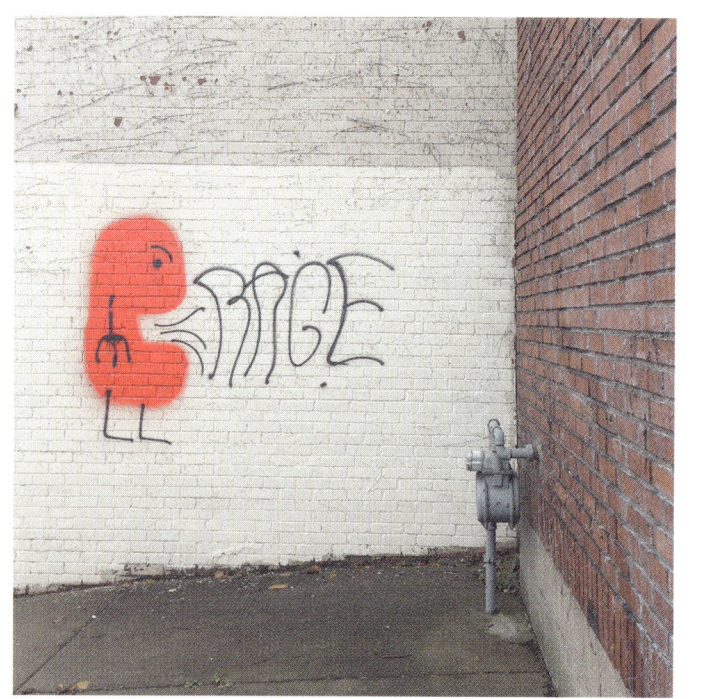
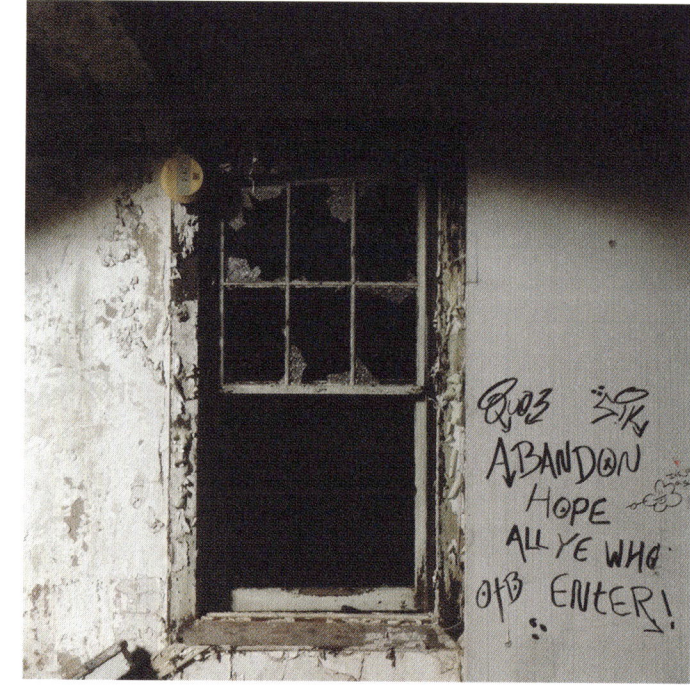

I'M JUST A PRINCE

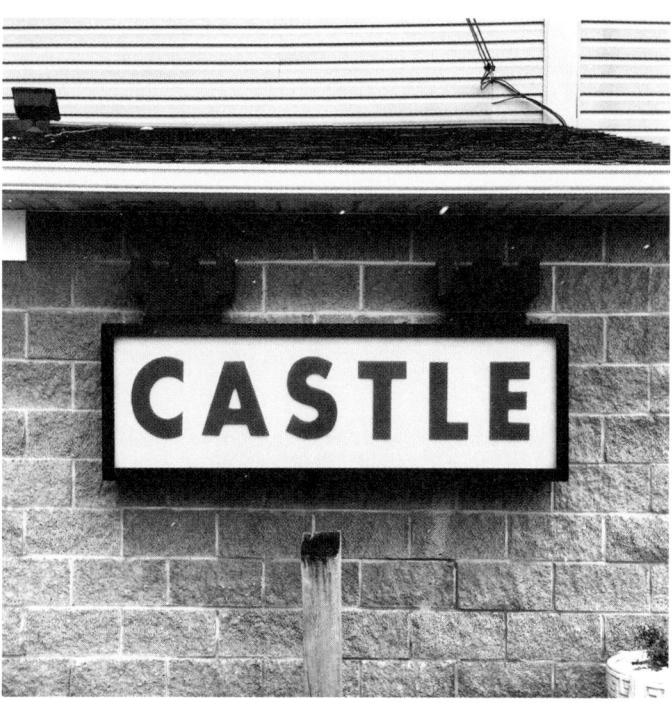

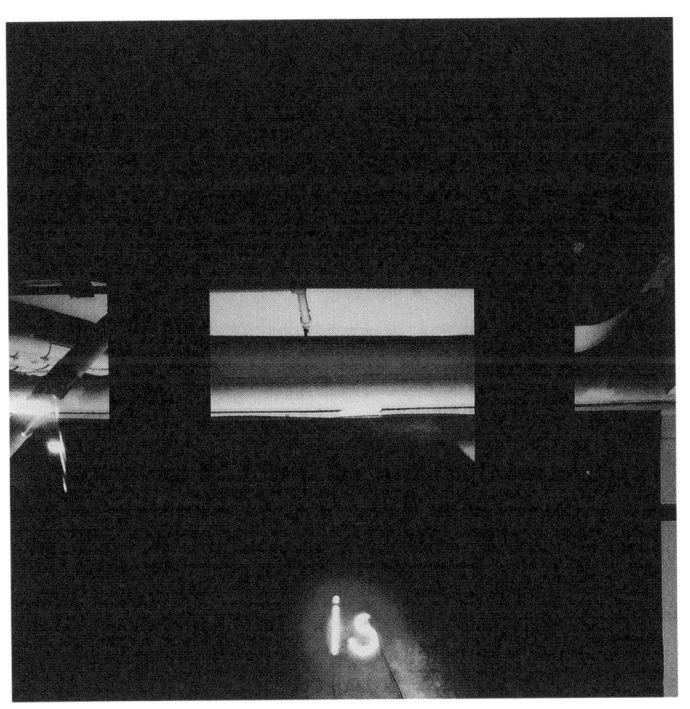

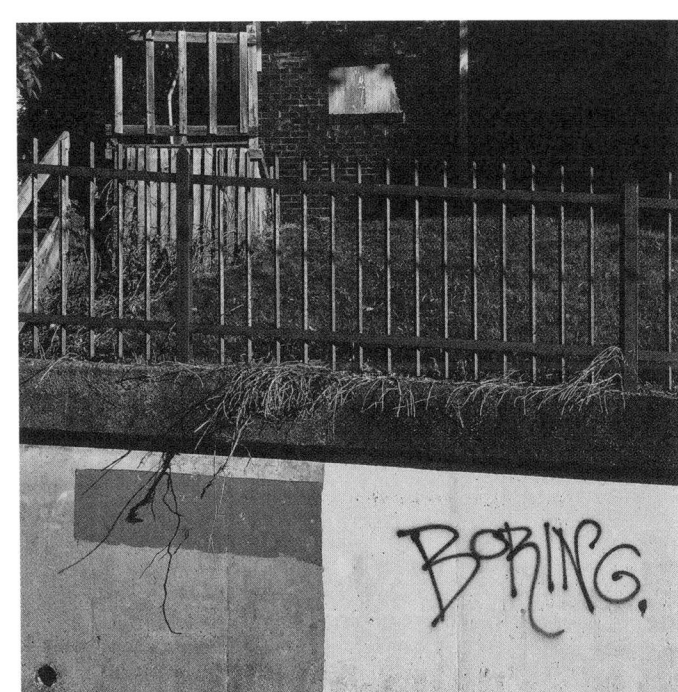

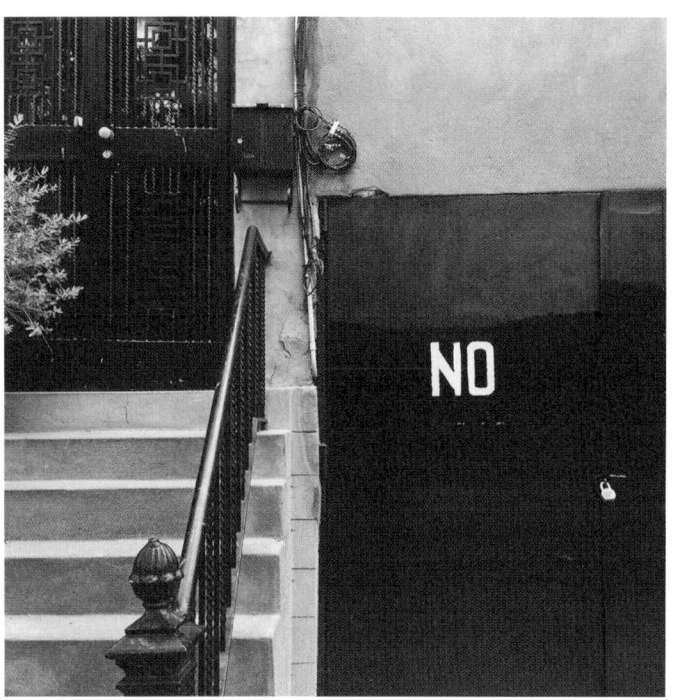
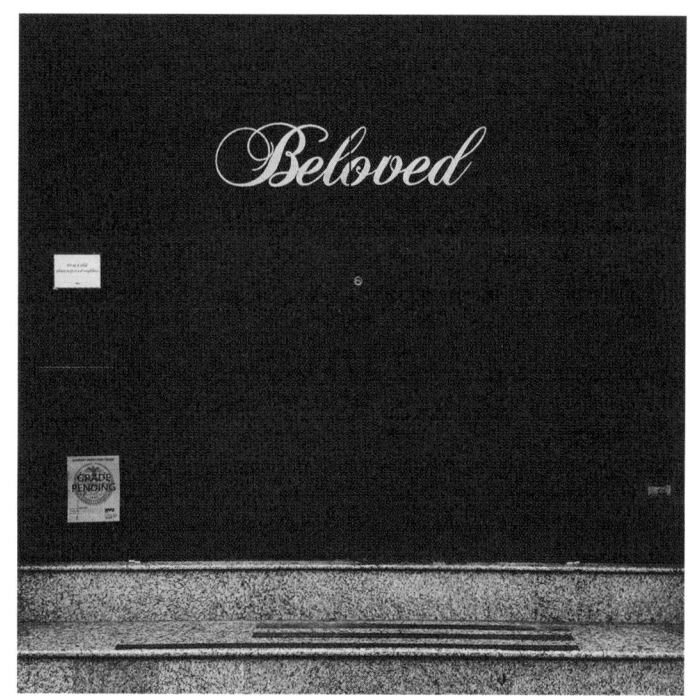

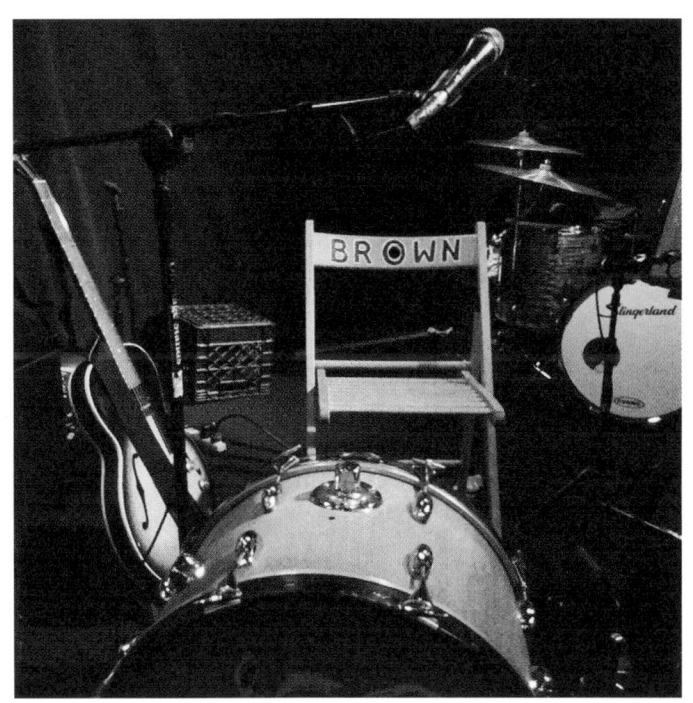

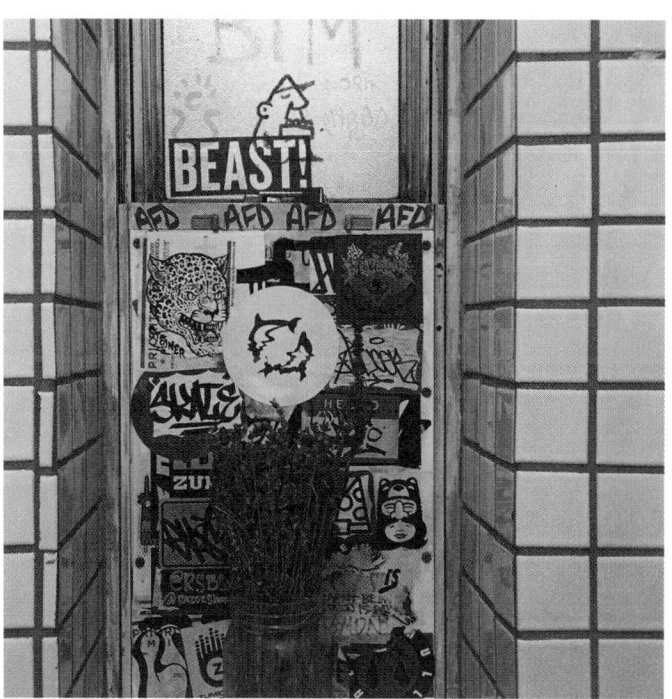

XOXO

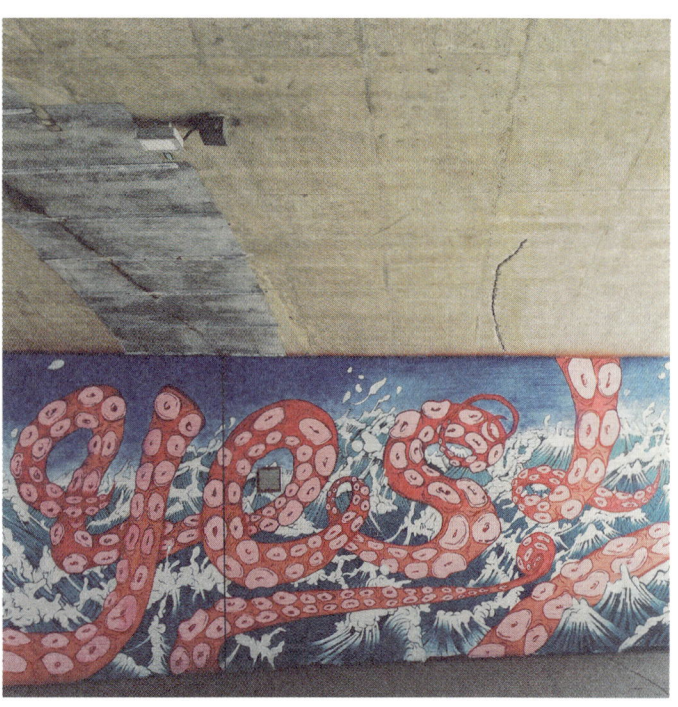

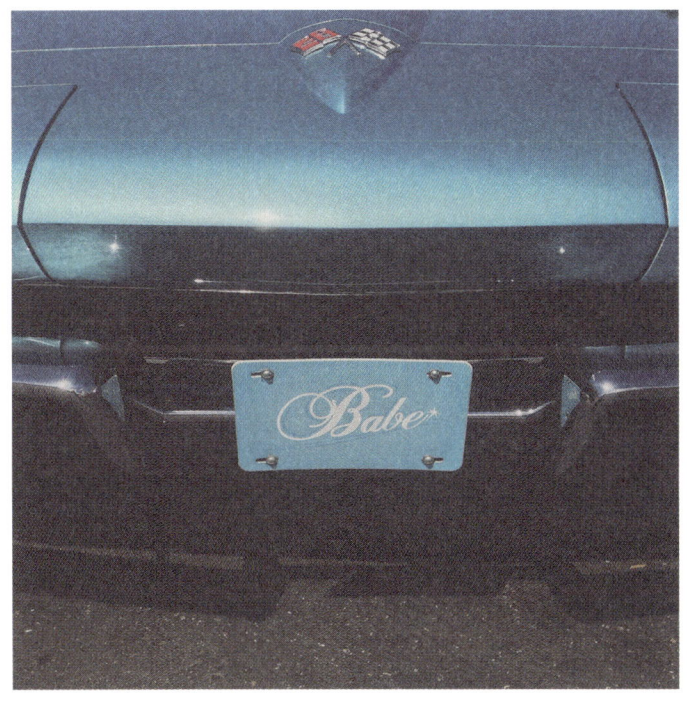

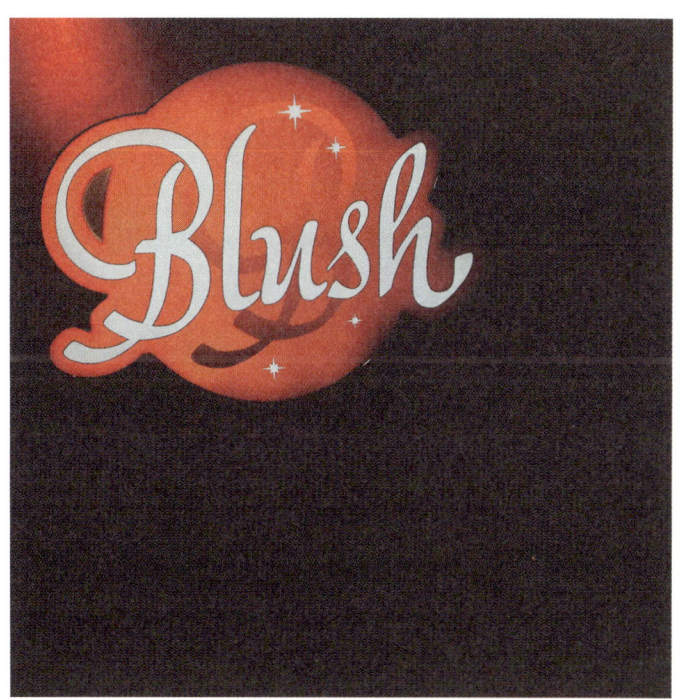

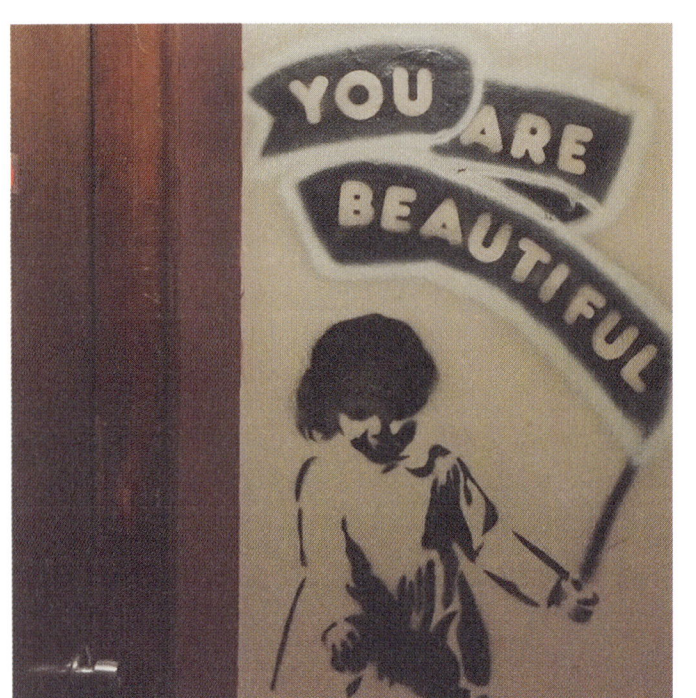
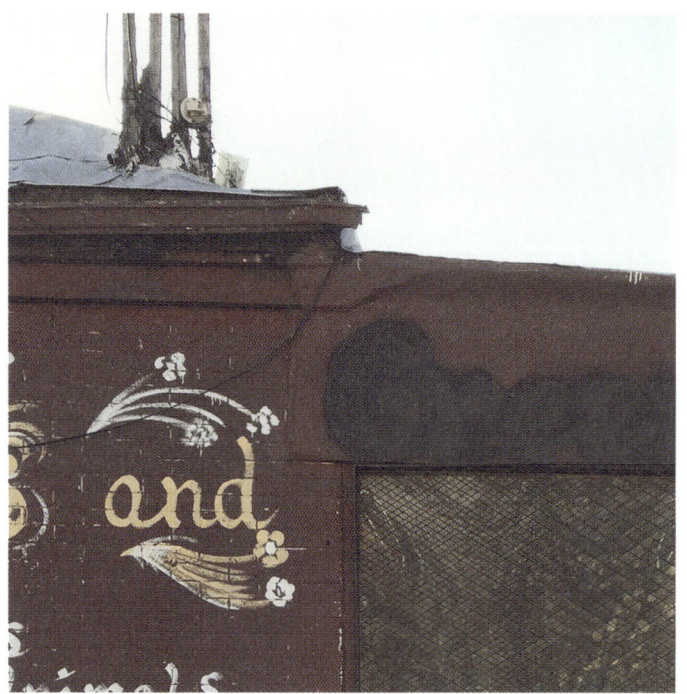

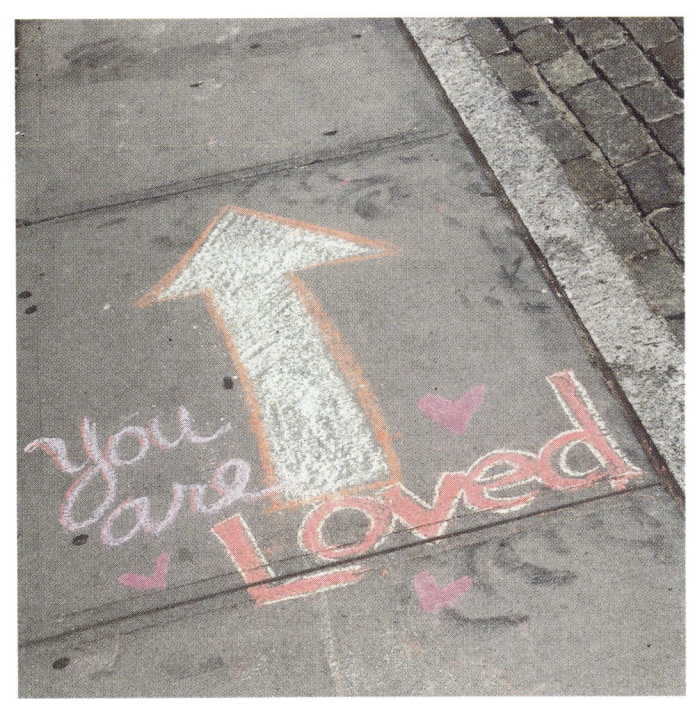

IT WOULDN'T FLUSH · FRANKS & BEANS · KNOCK TWICE
ASK FOR BOB · SEE ME AFTER CLASS · FAT & LAZY ·
SHOTGUN · WHEN I GROW UP · ONE EYE OPEN · CHAPTER
ONE · FREAK SHOW · THE DRUNK JOCKEY · REVELATION ·
JUST MARRIED · HAND IN HAND · GONE TOO SOON · OLD
& SENILE · FLIPPER FLIPPED OUT · PIT STOP · A REQUEST
FROM THE QUEEN · LAST GOODBYE · AND THEY'RE OFF ·
CHEFS SPECIAL · MIND LOST · MOTHER'S SECRET · CAGE
MATCH · I'M JUST A RANGE · XOXO · **QUITTING TIME**
· 96 YEARS YOUNG · ESCAPING REALITY · A NIGHT IN
LOVE · SUMMER IN RUSSIA · BUNKMATES · LOVE MOM ·
SLEEP TIGHT · LUNCH LADY REVENGE · FUTURE FEARS
· ON BROADWAY · AT FIRST SITE · NATURE CHANNEL ·
FAIRYTALES · TIME TO RUN · IN THE STREETS

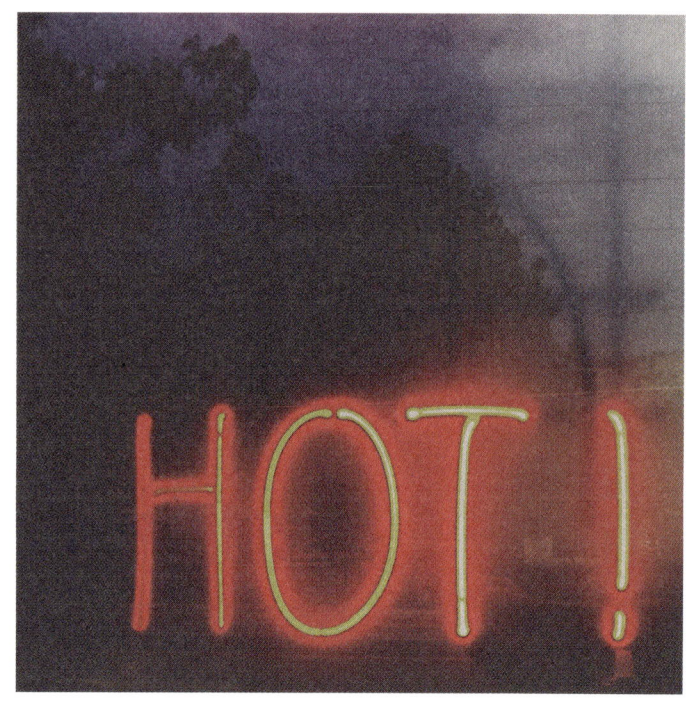

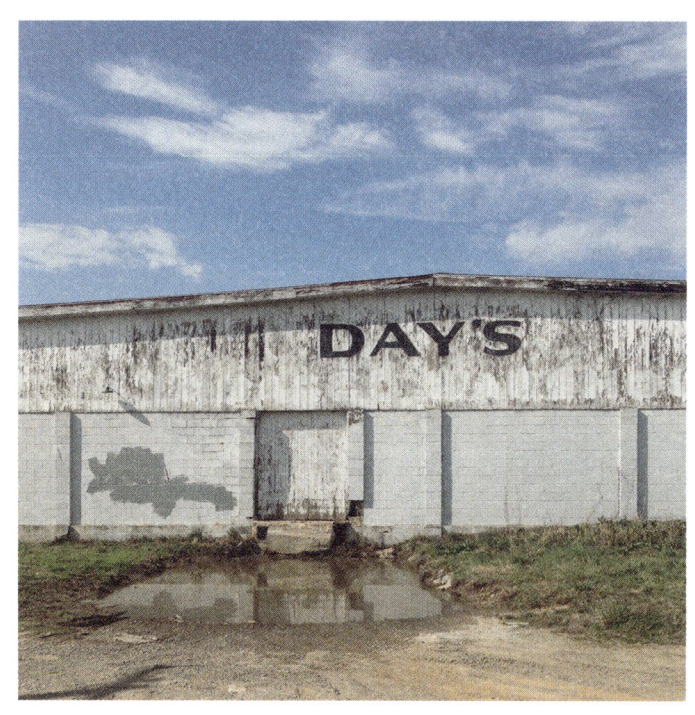

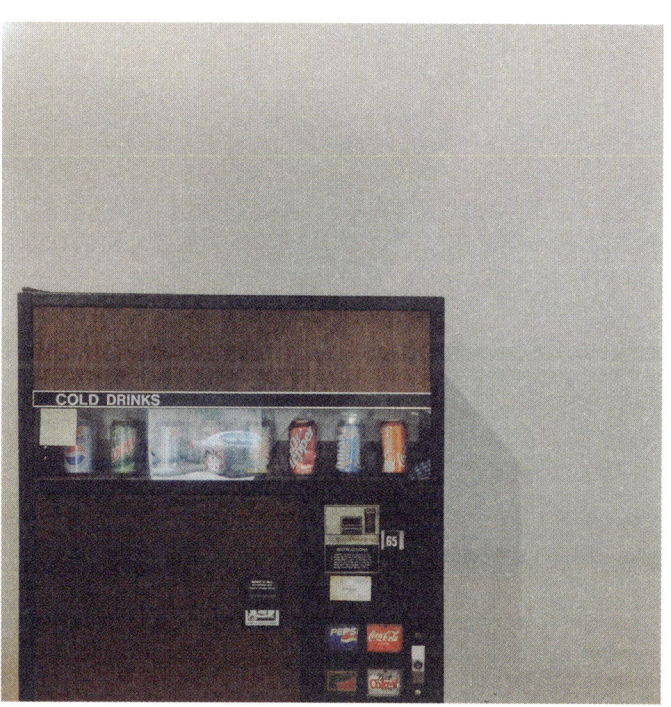

86 YEARS YOUNG

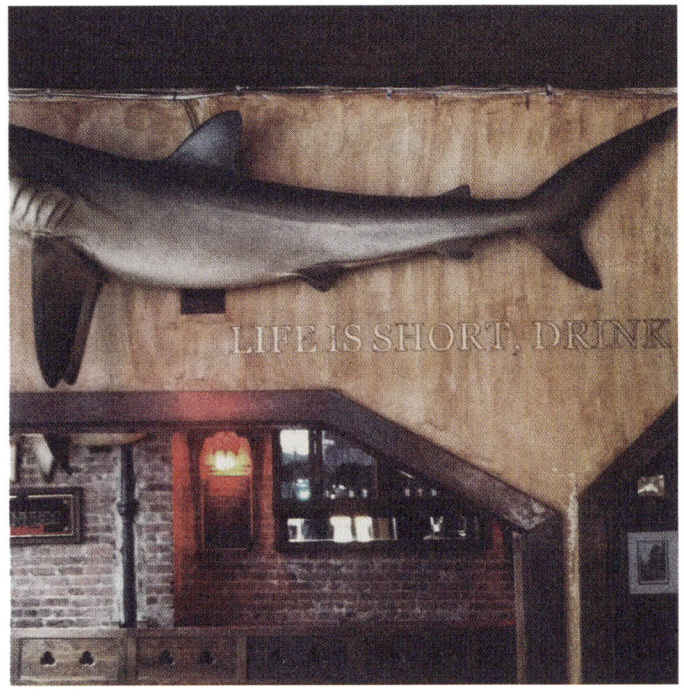

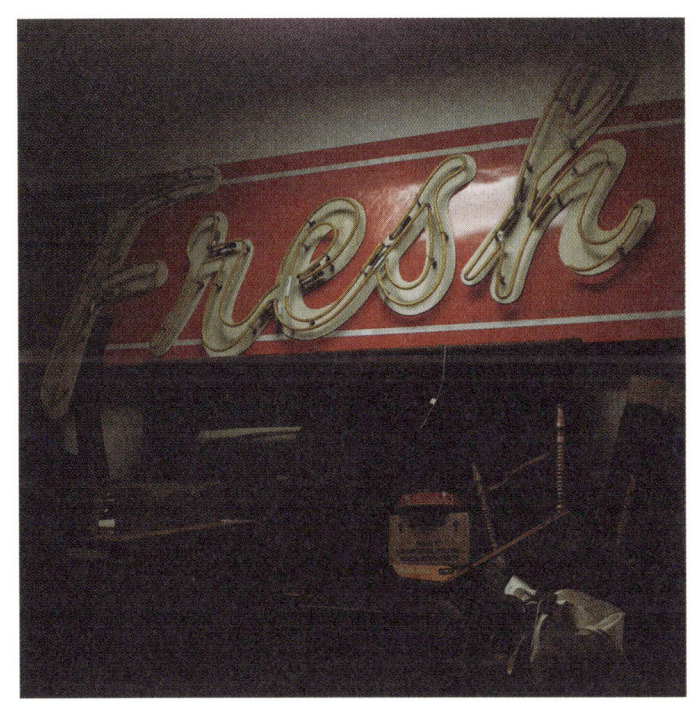
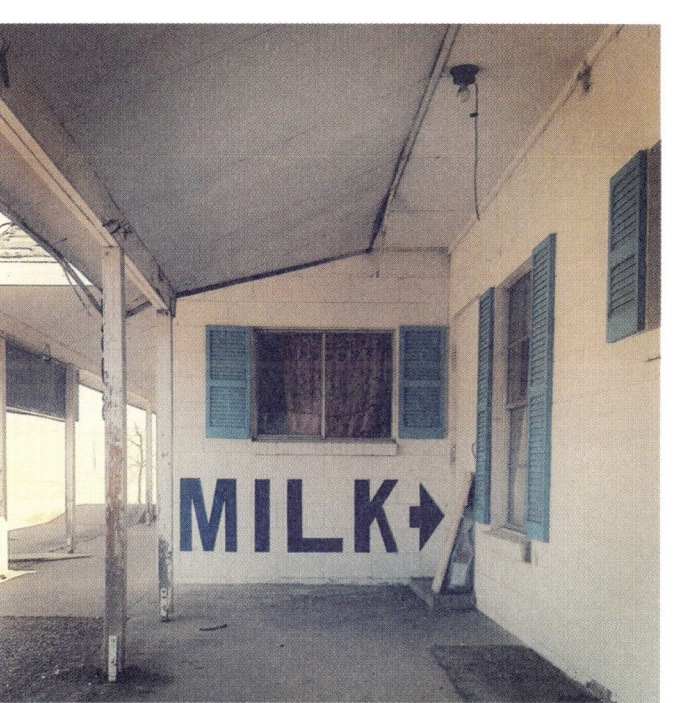

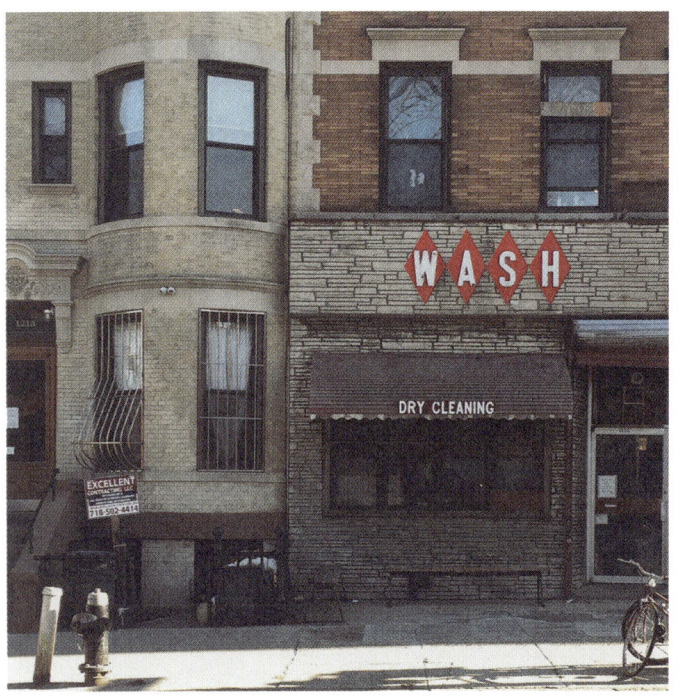
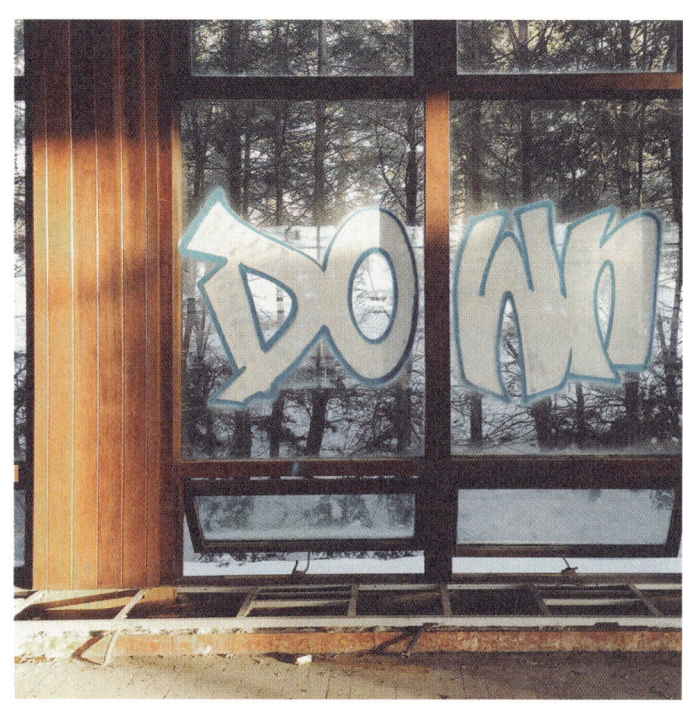

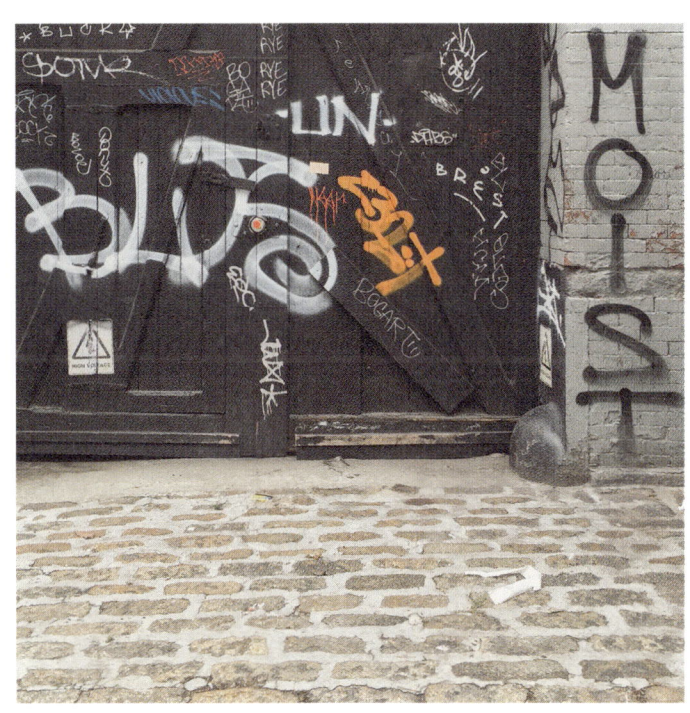
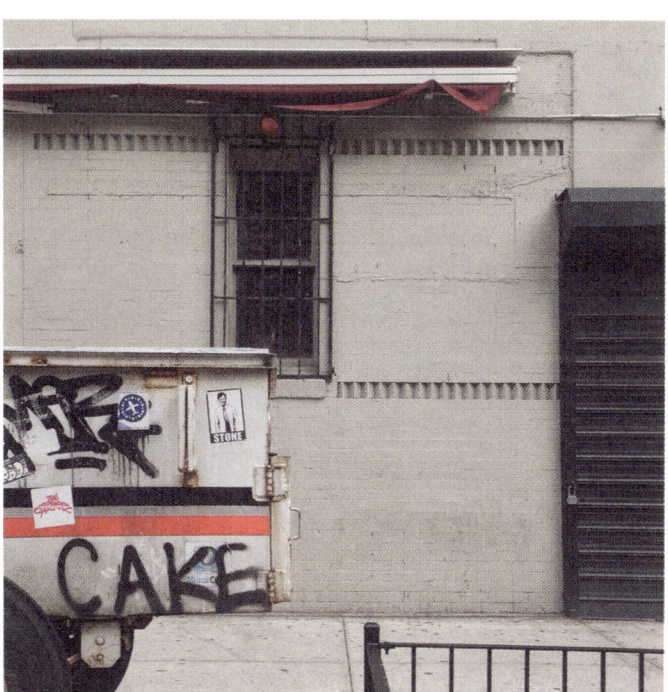

ESCAPING REALITY

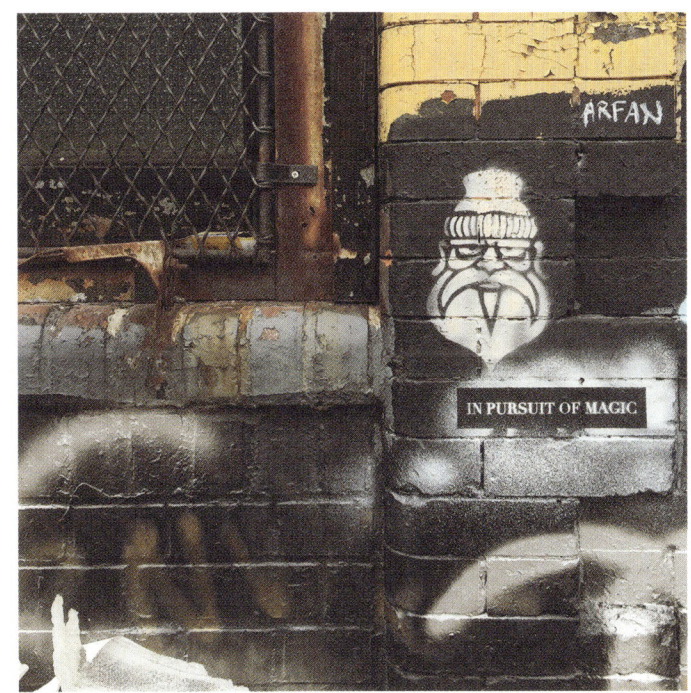

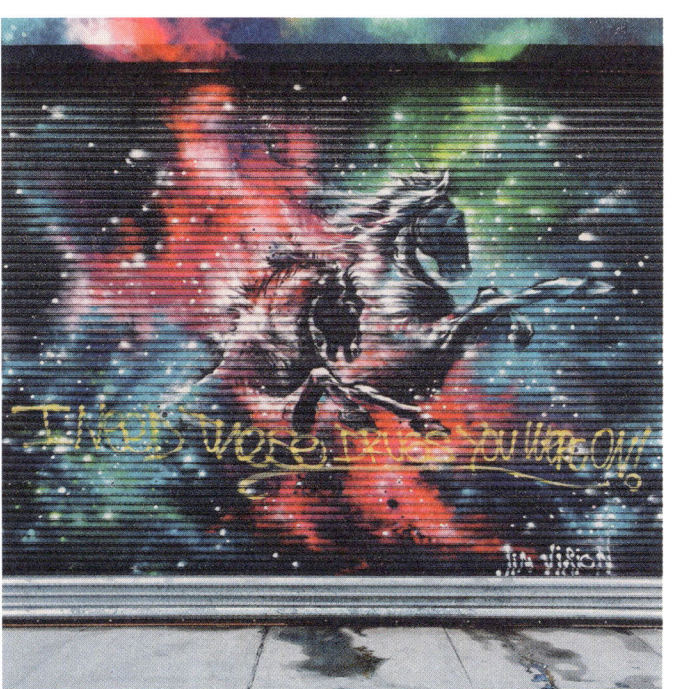

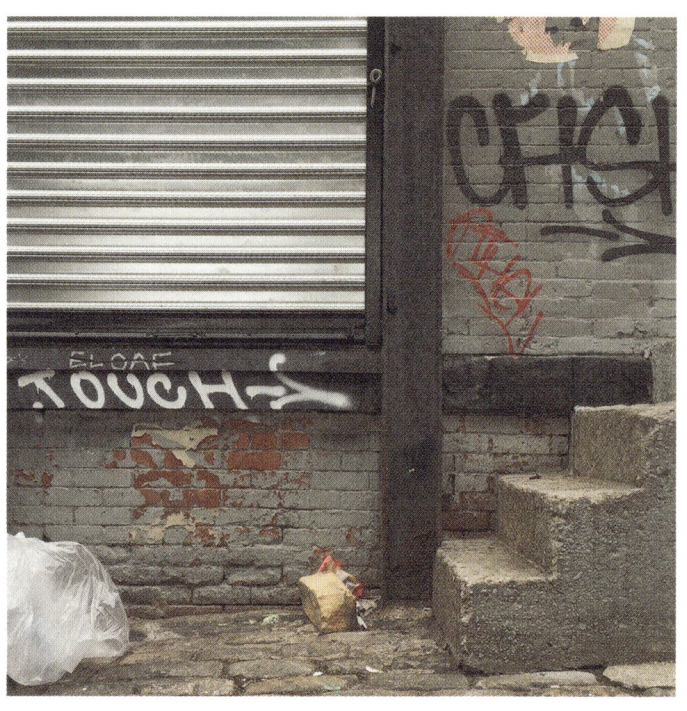

IT WOULDN'T FLUSH · FRANKS & BEANS · KNOCK TWICE · ASK FOR BOB · SEE ME AFTER CLASS · FAT & LAZY · SHOTGUN · WHEN I GROW UP · ONE EYE OPEN · CHAPTER ONE · FREAK SHOW · THE DRUNK JOCKEY · REVELATION · LOST WEEKEND · HANDLE WITH CARE · HOME SWEET HOME · OLD & WISER · FLIPPER FLIPPED OUT · BIG STUFF · A REQUEST FROM THE QUEEN · LAST GOODBYE · AND THEN WE ARE GONE · CHECK CENTRAL · KING LOST · MOTHER'S SECRET · SAFE HATCH · I'M JILL'S PRINCE · XOXO · QUITTING TIME · BE YOUNG, YOUNG · ESCAPING REALITY ·

A NIGHT IN LOVE · DINNER IN RUSSIA · BUNKMATES · LOVE, MOM · CLEAR SIGHT · DANCE · AIN REVENGE · FUTURE FEARS · ON BROADWAY · AT FIRST SITE · NATURE CHANNEL · FAIRYTALES · TIME TO RUN · IN THE STREETS

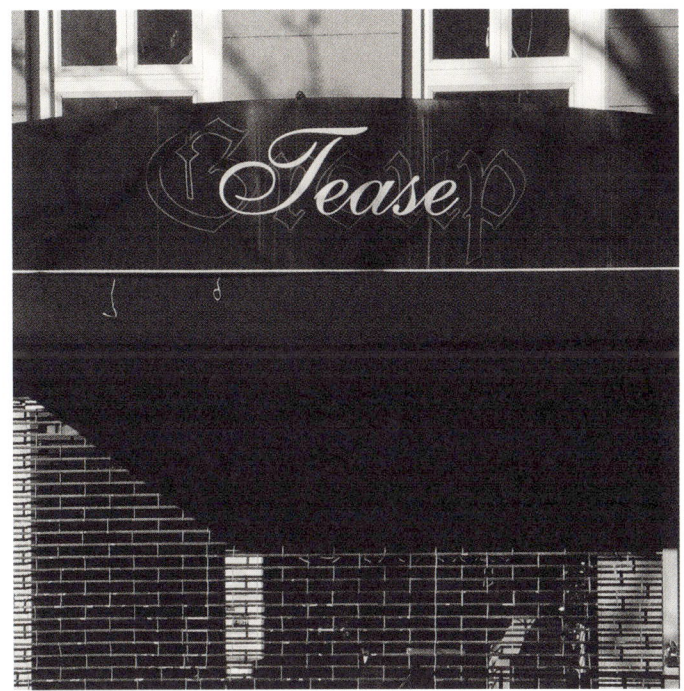
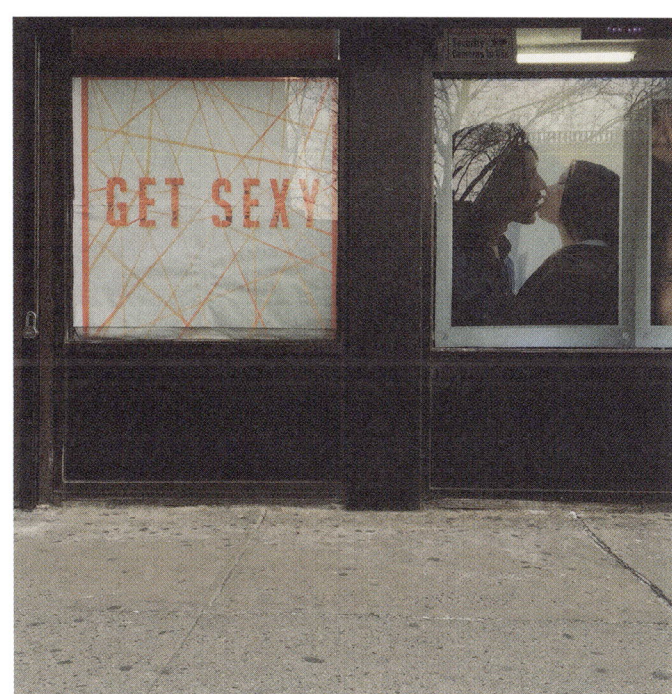

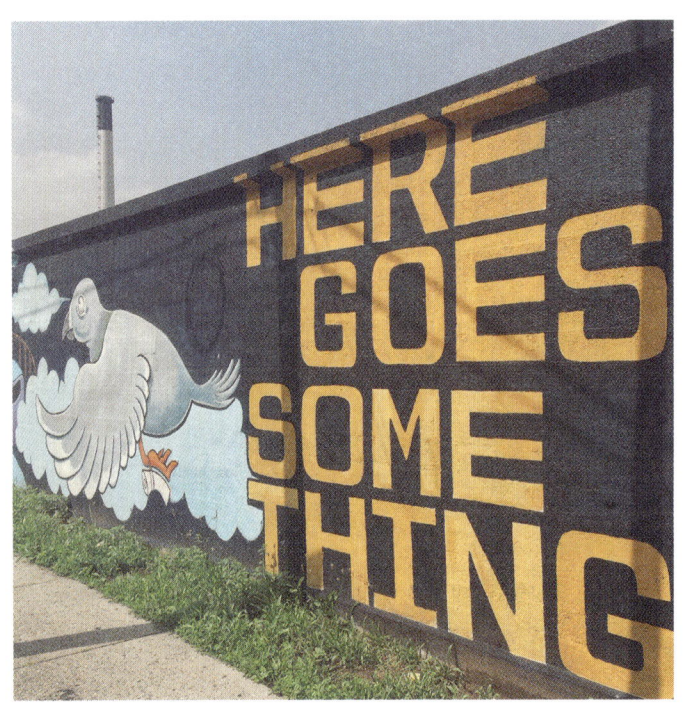
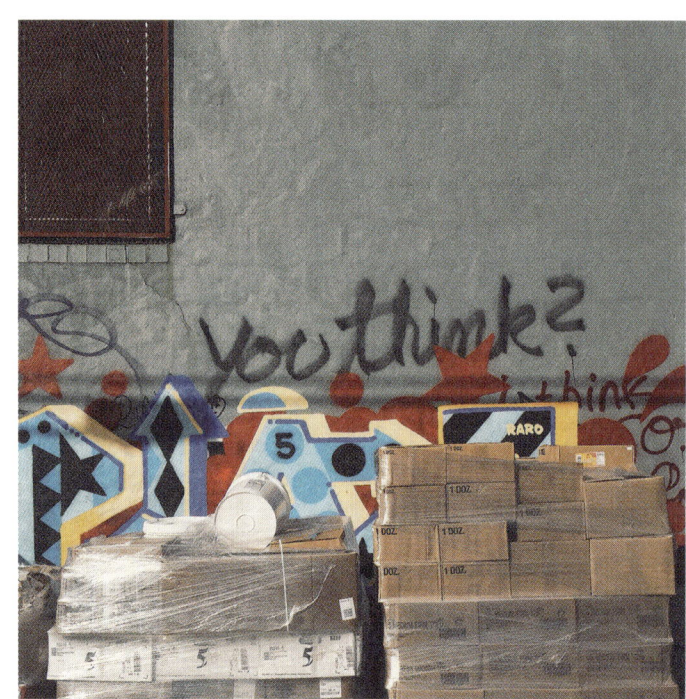

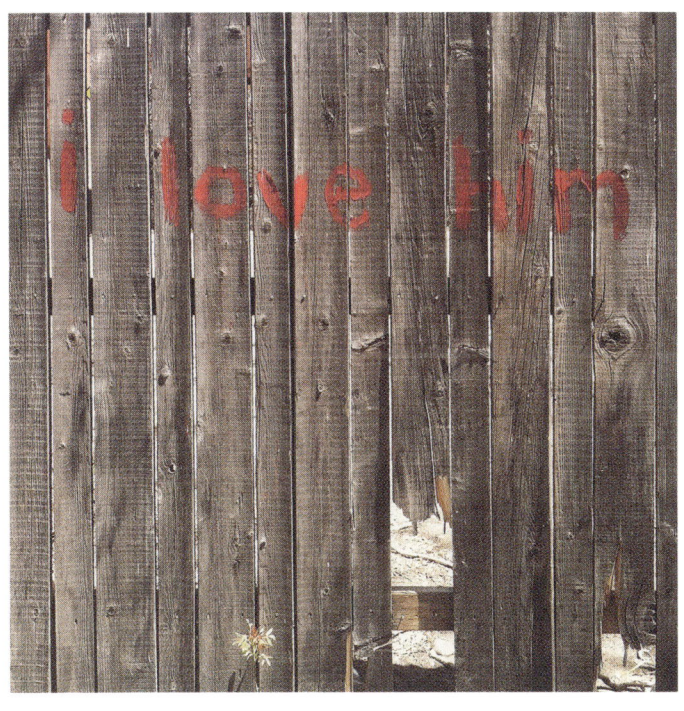

SUMMER IN RUSSIA

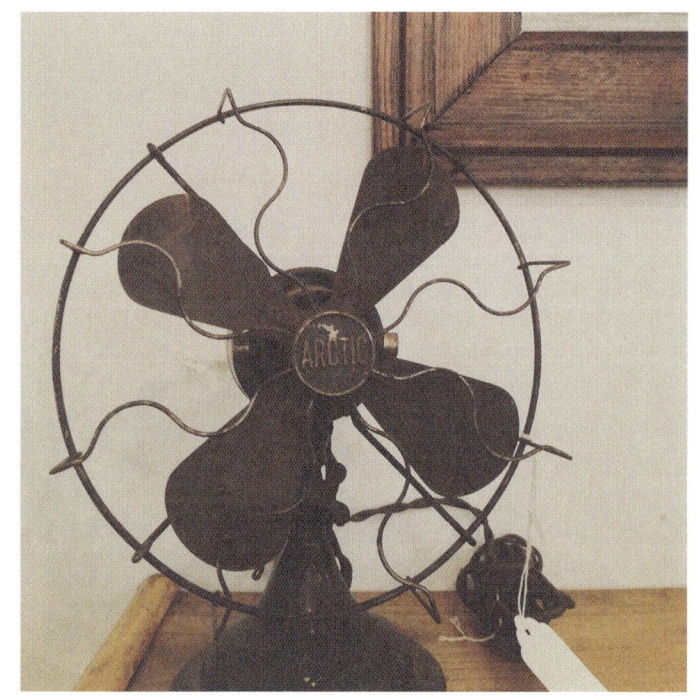

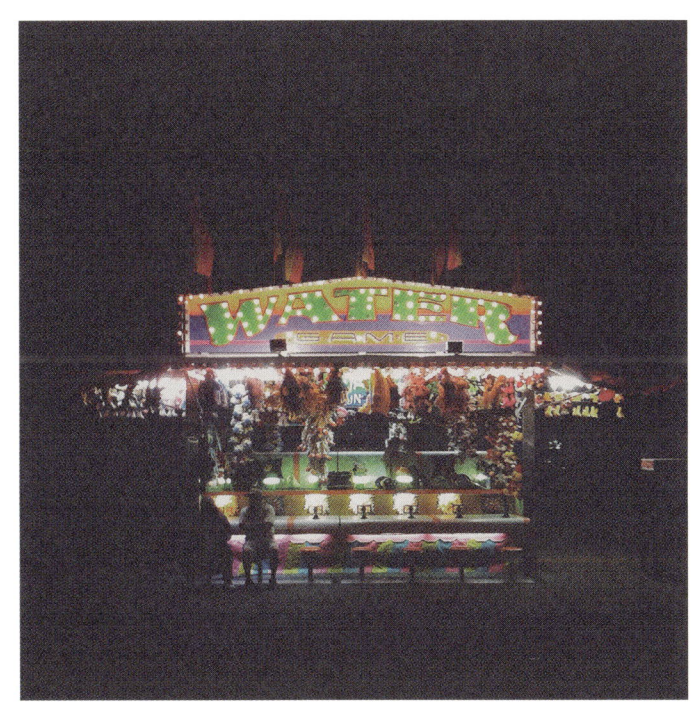
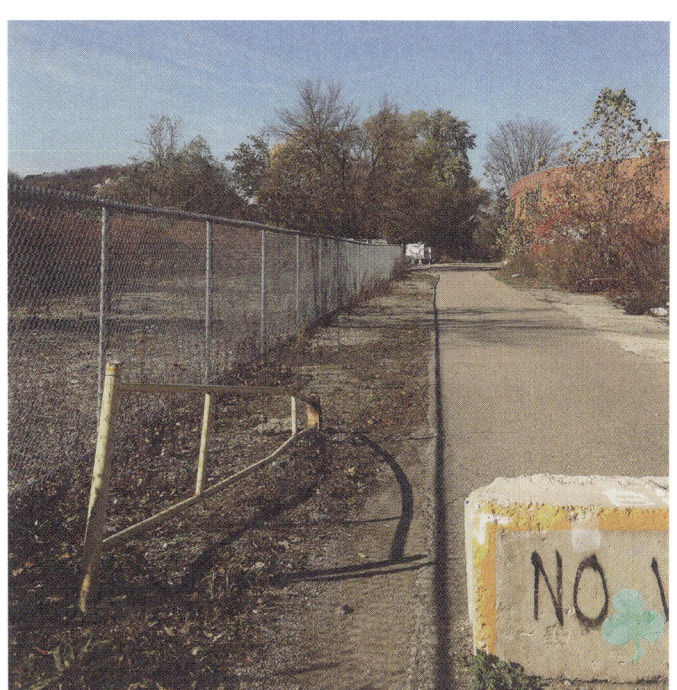

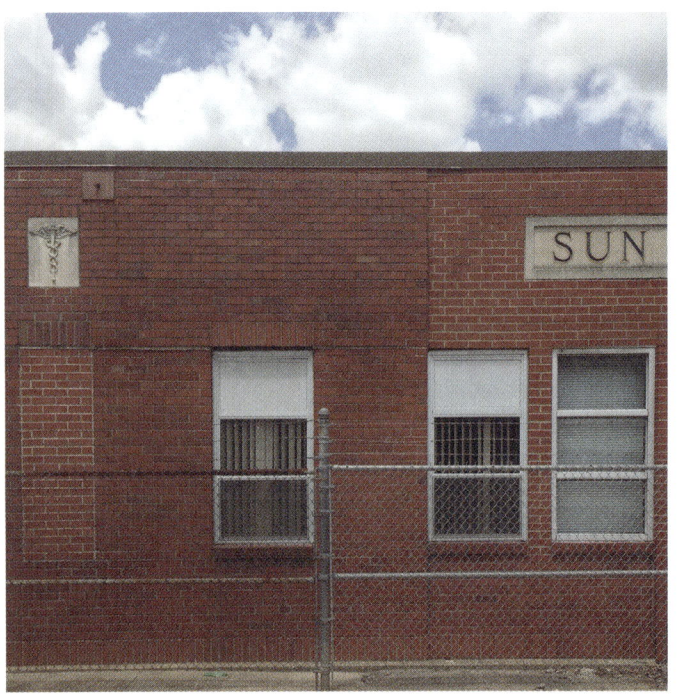
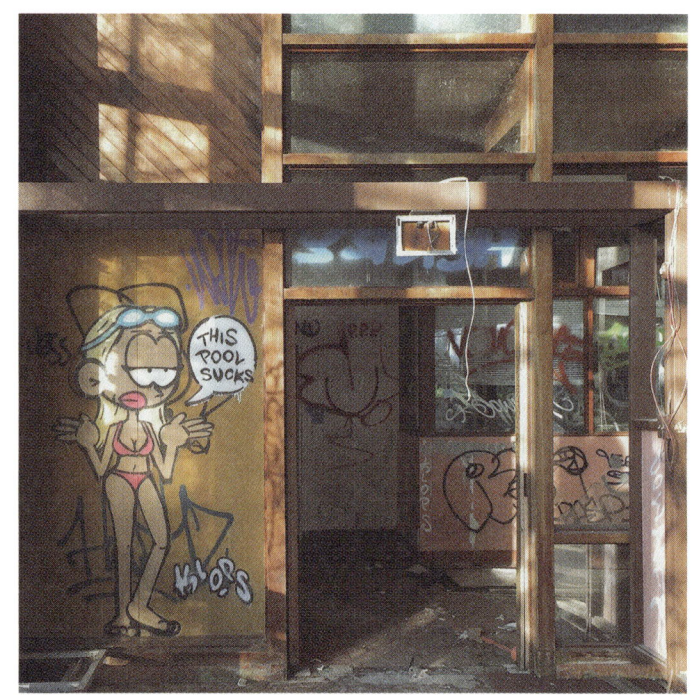

BUNKMATES

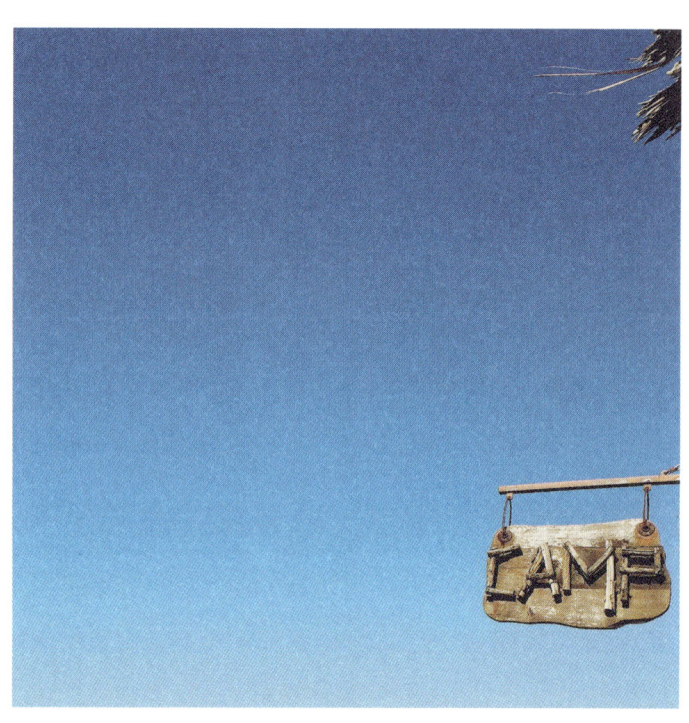

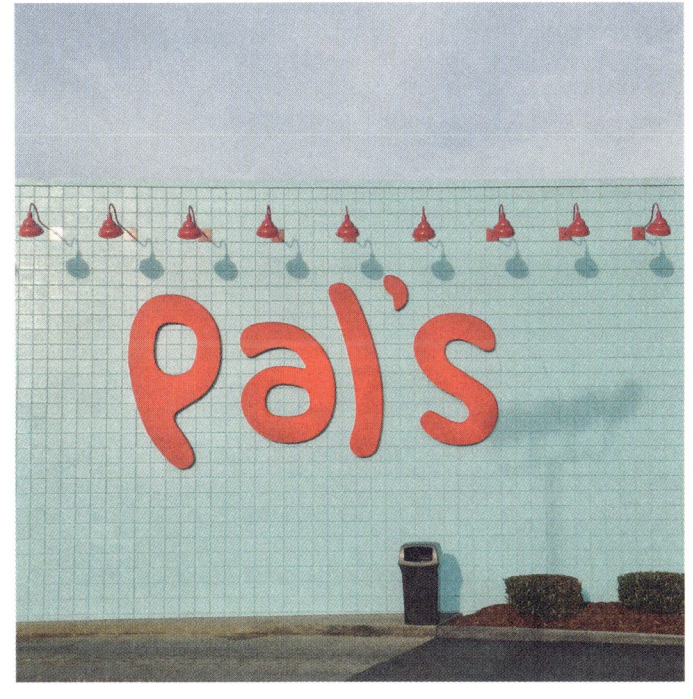

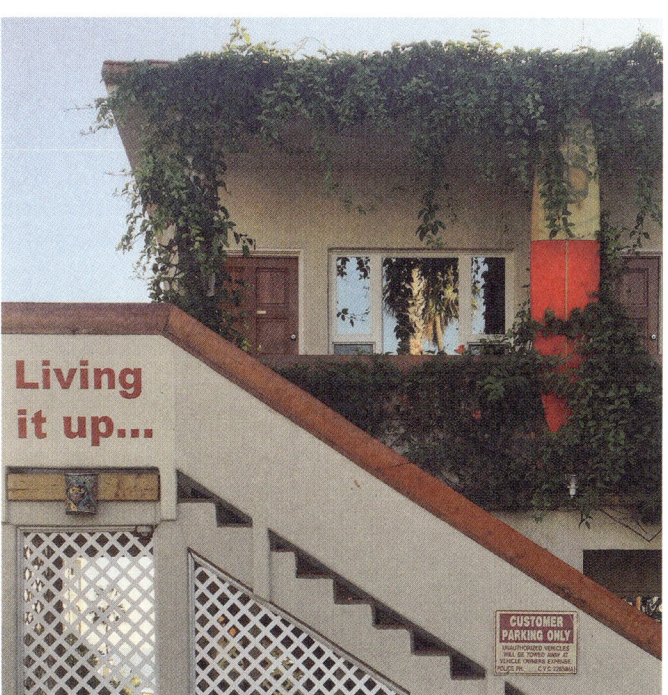

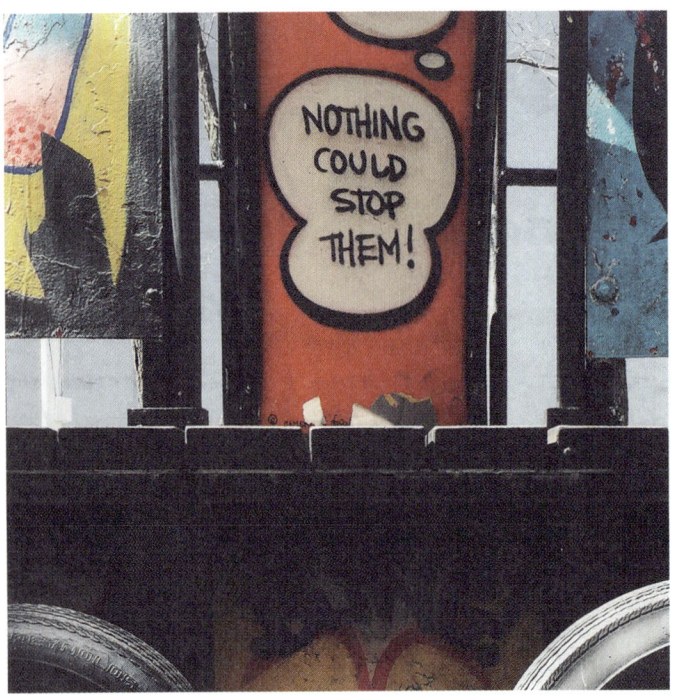
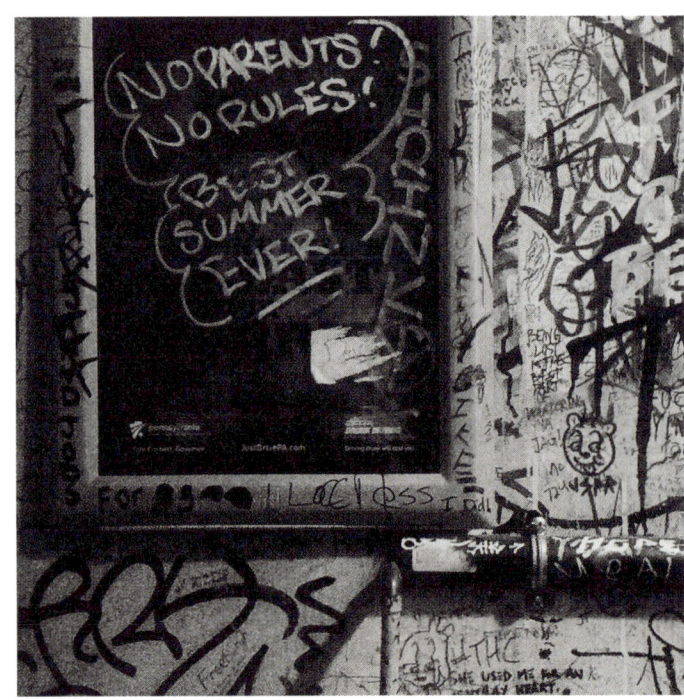

LOVE, MOM

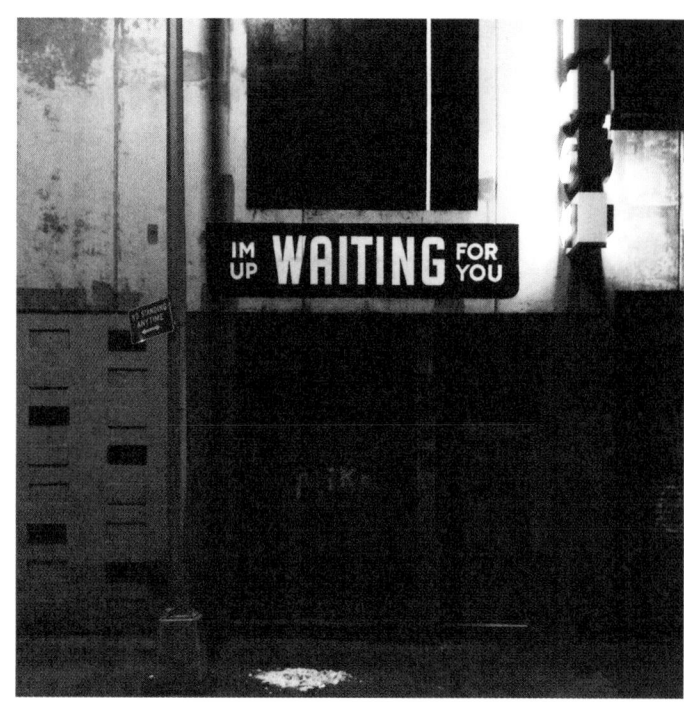

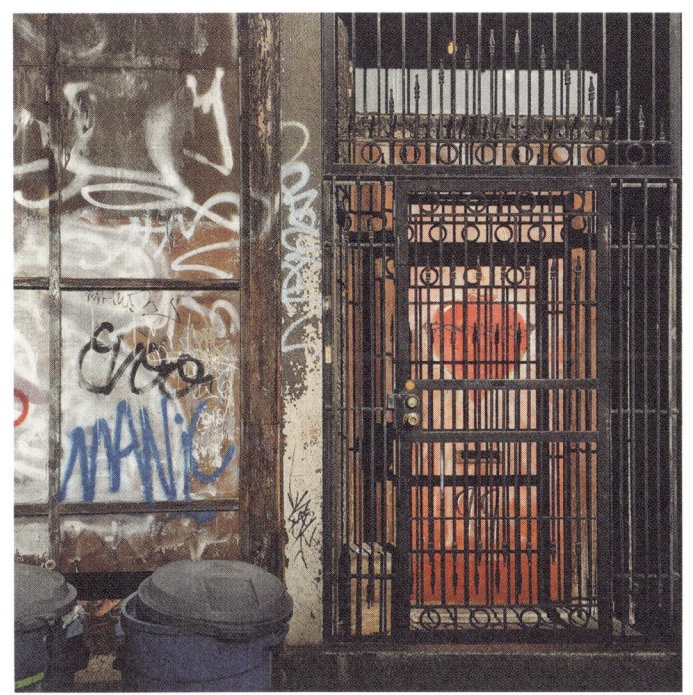
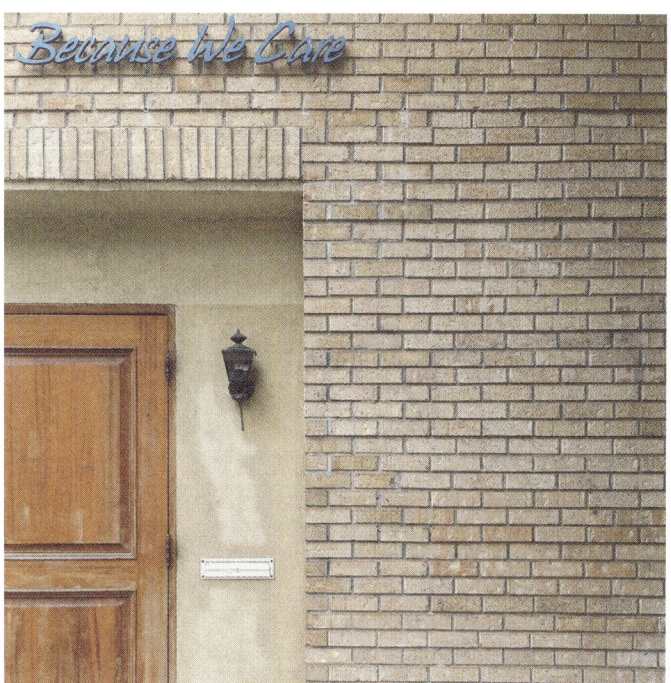

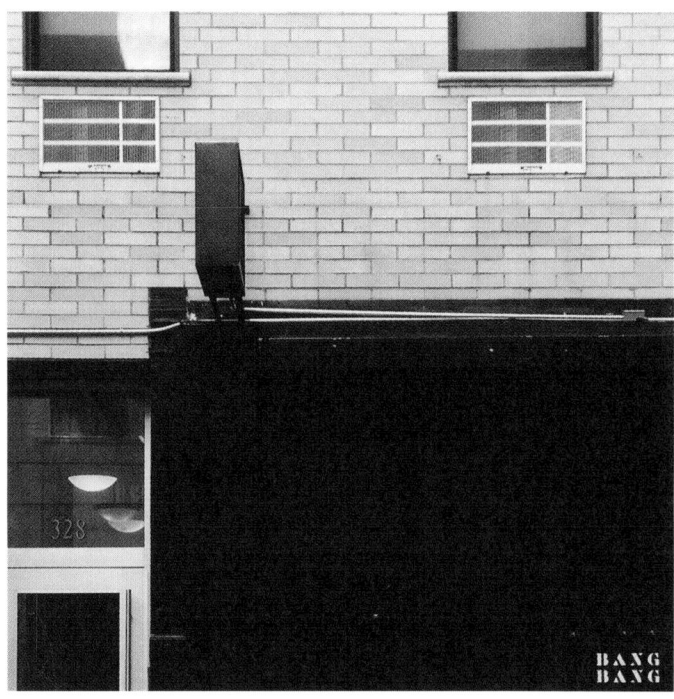

IT WOULDN'T FLUSH · FRANKS & BEANS · KNOCK TWICE · ASK FOR MOM · SEE ME AFTER CLASS · FAT & LAZY · SHOTGUN · WHEN I GROW UP · ONE EYE OPEN · CHAPTER ONE · FREAK SHOW · THE DRUNK JOCKEY · REVELATION · JUST MARRIED · HAND IN HAND · GONE · OH SNOW · U.F.O. · B SIDES · UPPER FLOORS ONLY · PIT STOP · A REQUEST FROM THE QUEEN · LAST GOODBYE · AND THEY'RE OFF · THIEF'S SPECIAL · LONG LOST · MOTHER'S SECRET · BACK PATCH · I'M JUST A DRINK · XOXO · BEDTIME STORY · 88 YEARS YOUNG · LEARNING BERLIN · A NIGHT IN LOVE · SUMMER IN RUSSIA · O WHAT'S IT · LOVE, MOM ·

SLEEP TIGHT · LUNCH LADY REVENGE · THOUSAND YEARS · ON BROADWAY · AT FIRST SITE · NATION LEARNING · FAIRYTALES · TIME TO RUN · IN THE STREETS

BANG
BANG

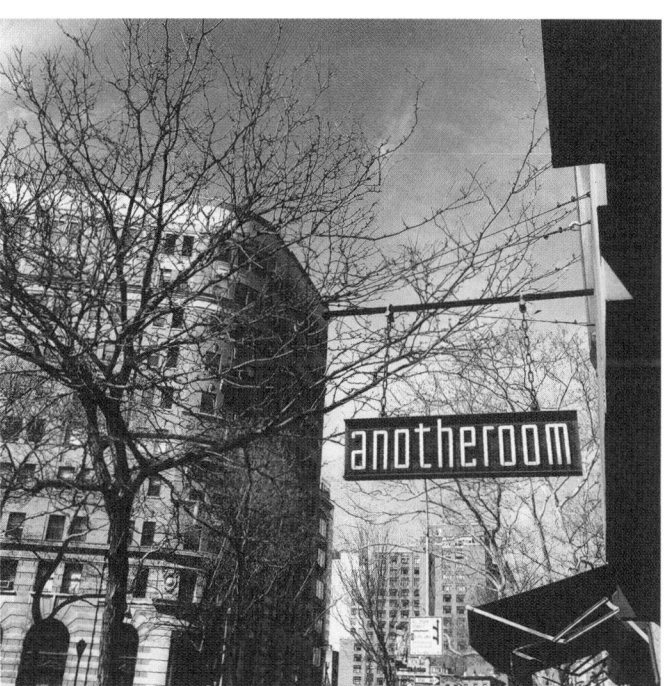

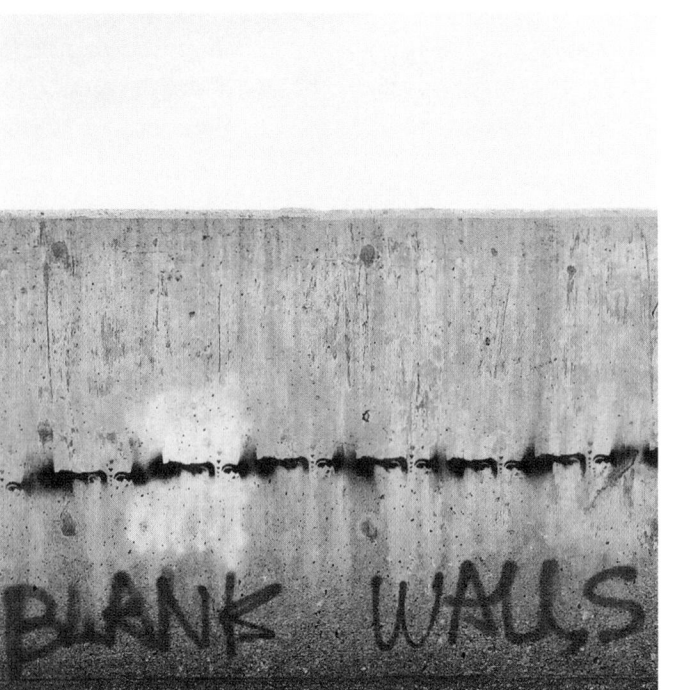
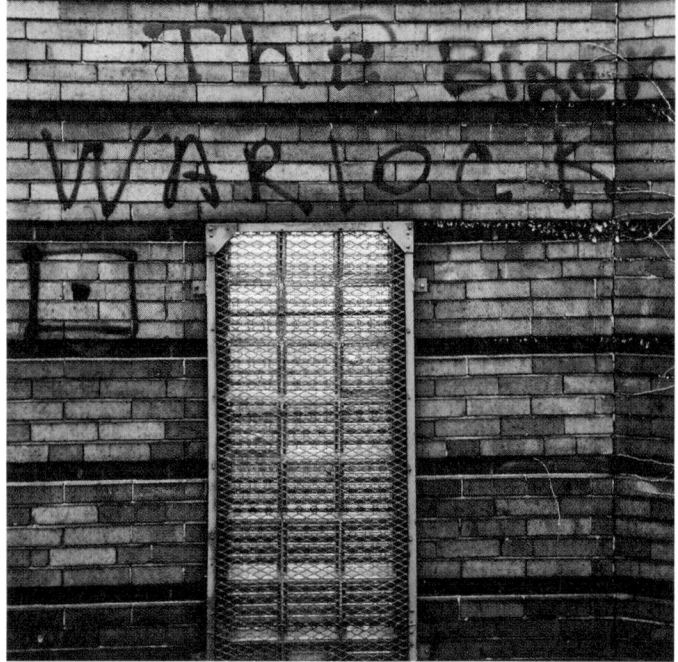

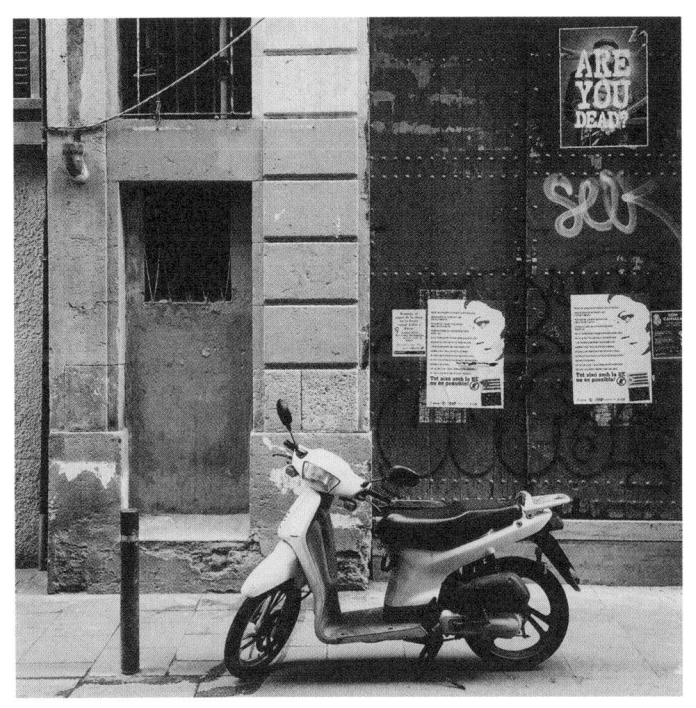

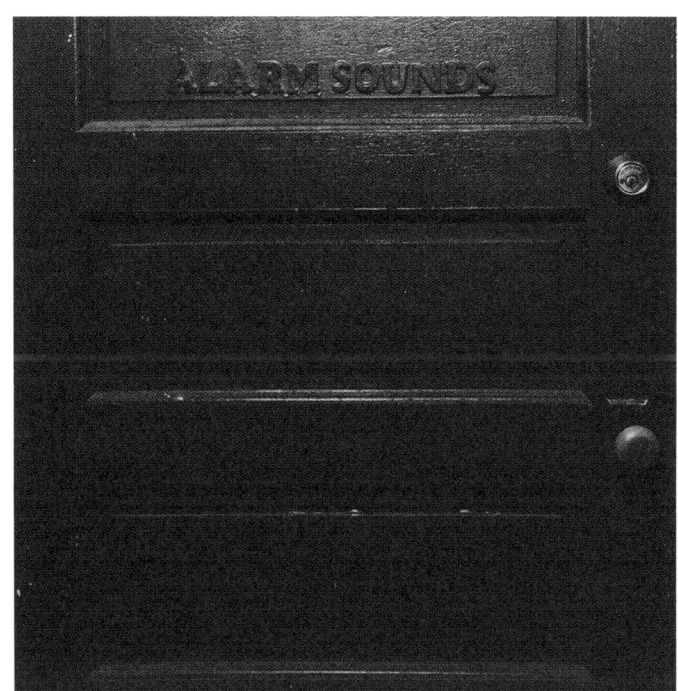

LUNCH LADY REVENGE

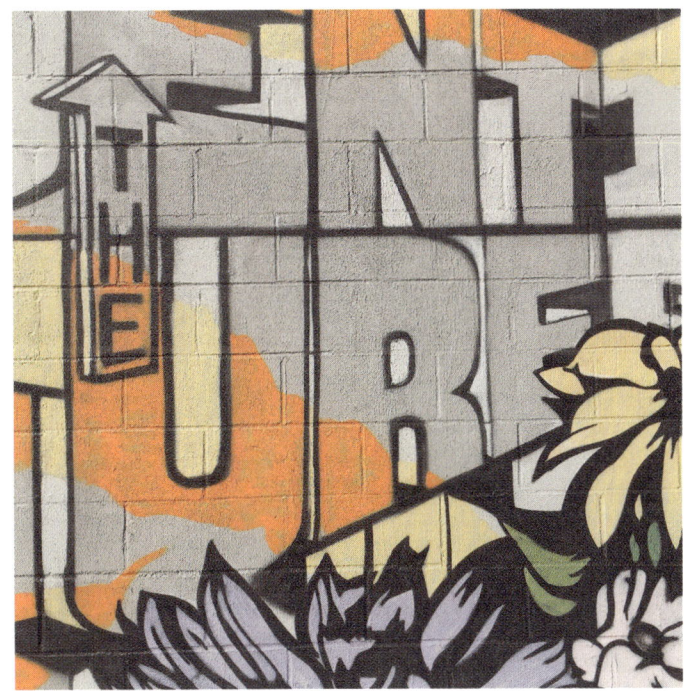

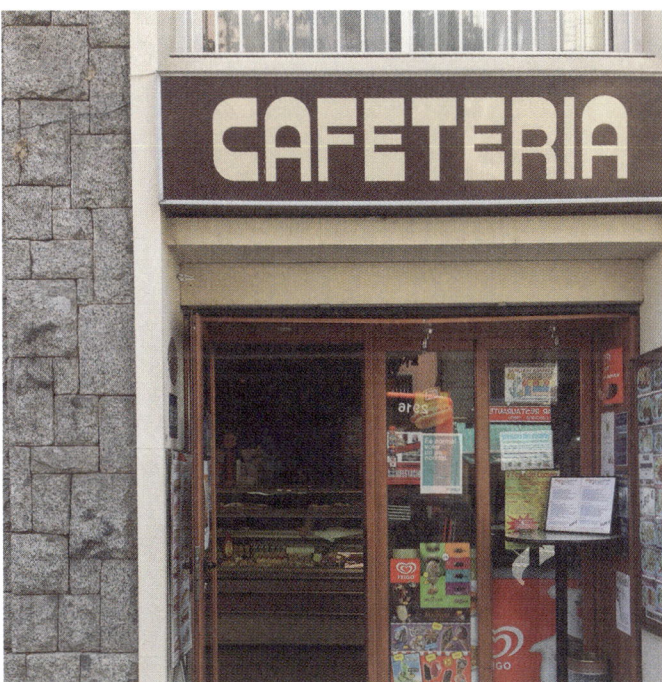

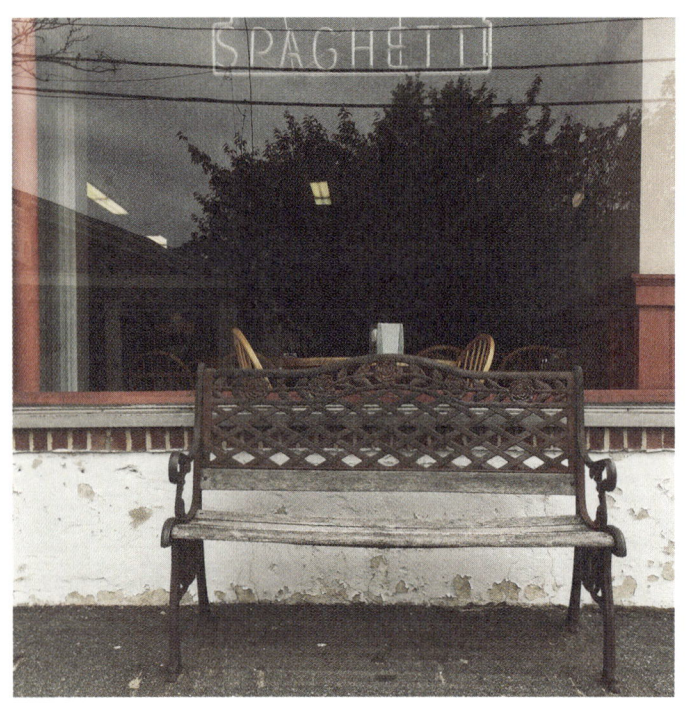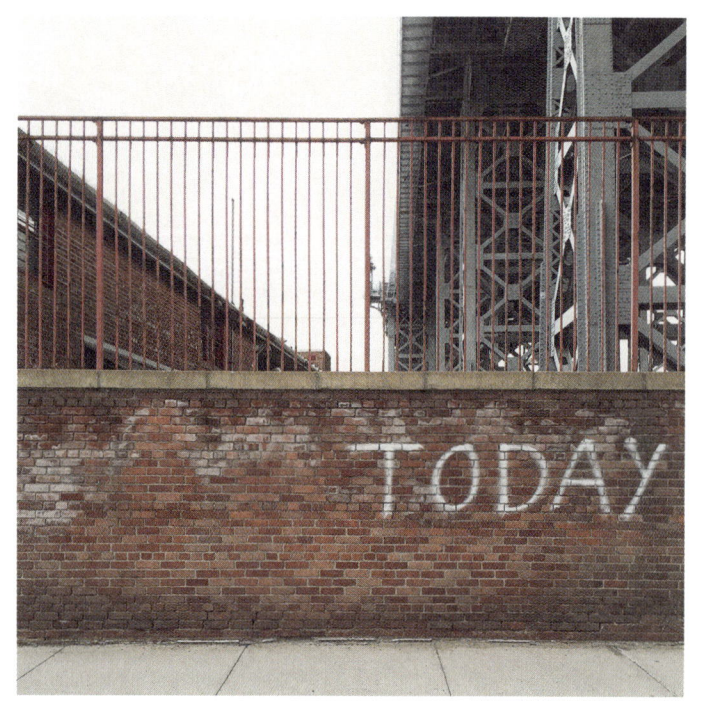

FUTURE FEARS

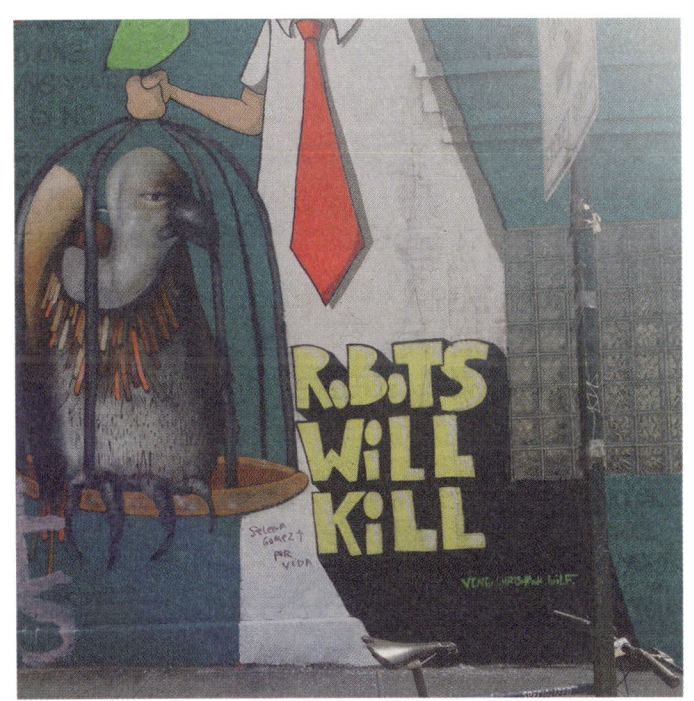

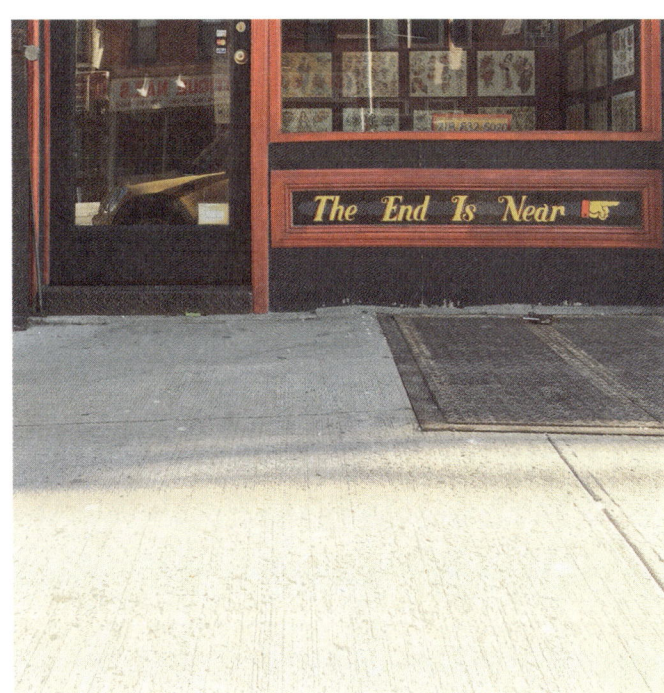

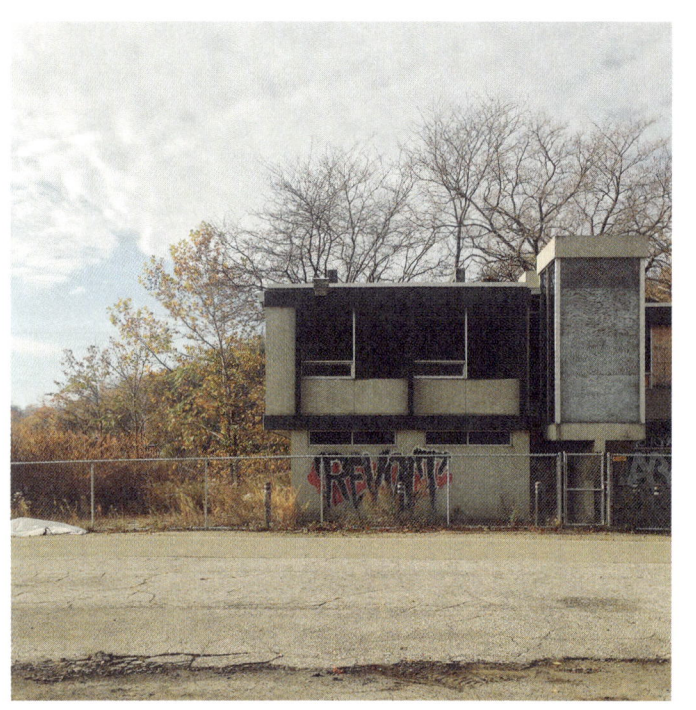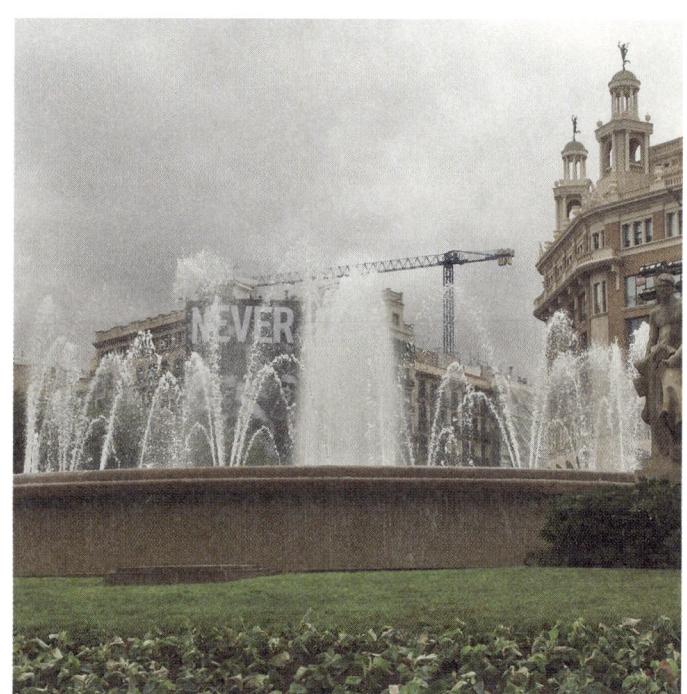

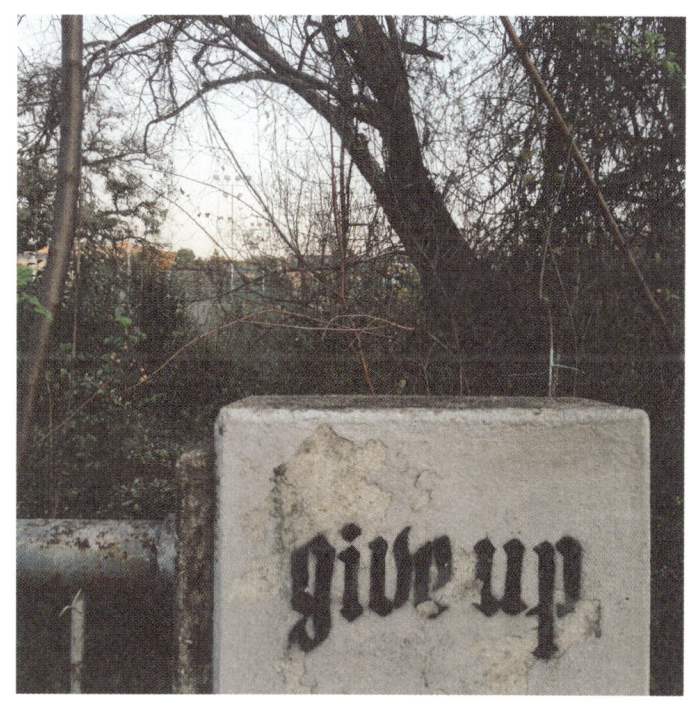

ON BROADWAY

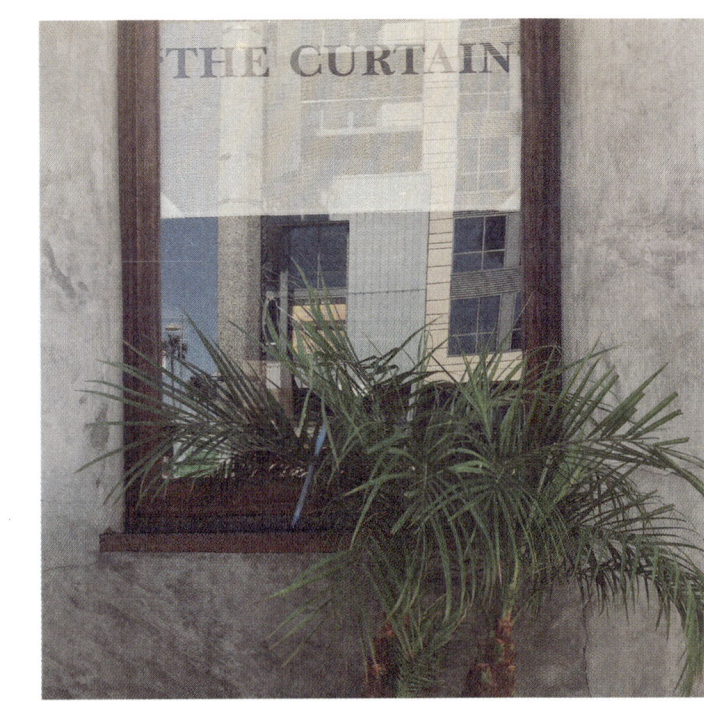

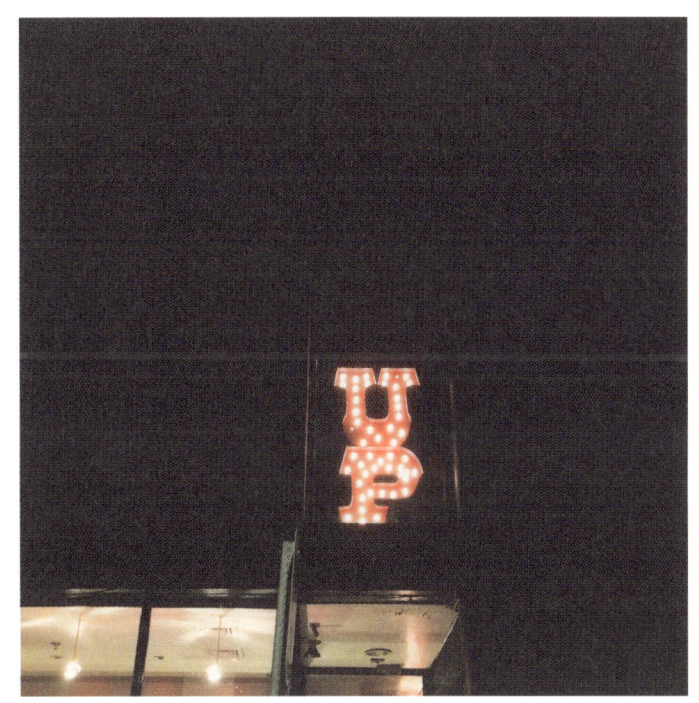

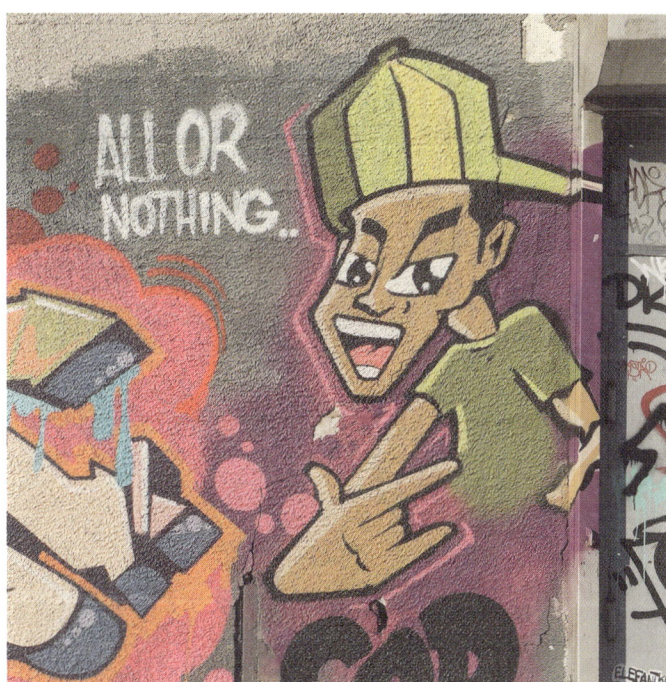

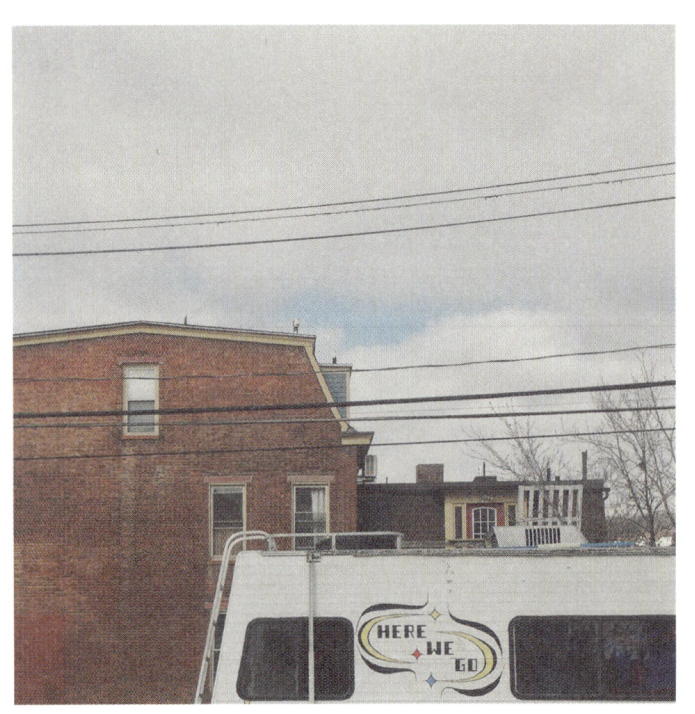

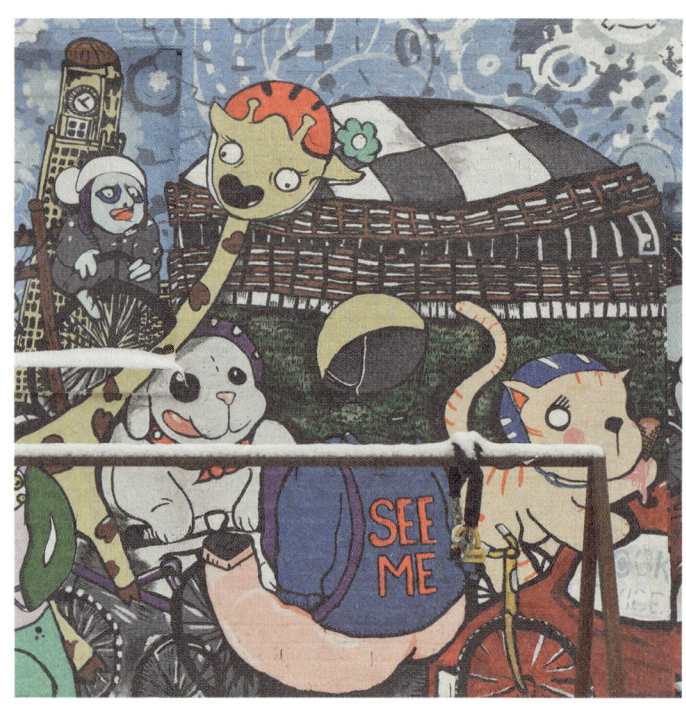

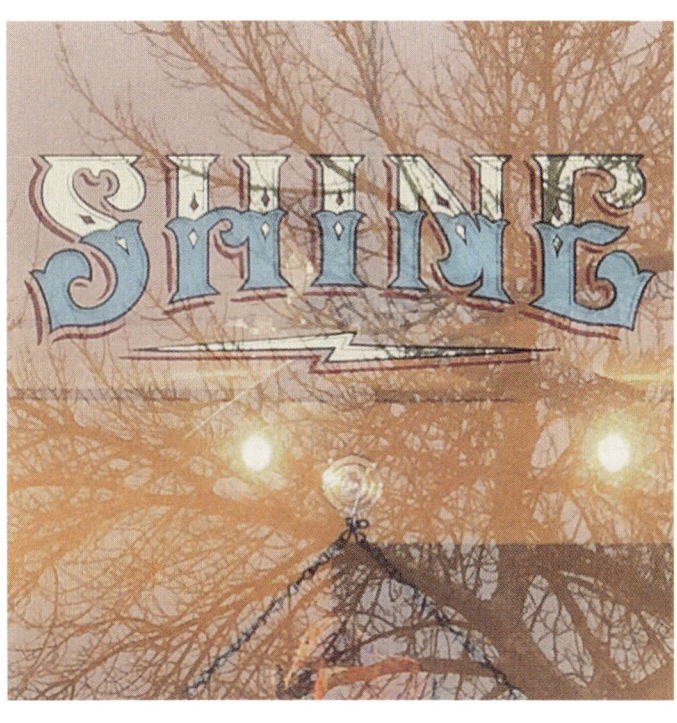

AT FIRST SITE

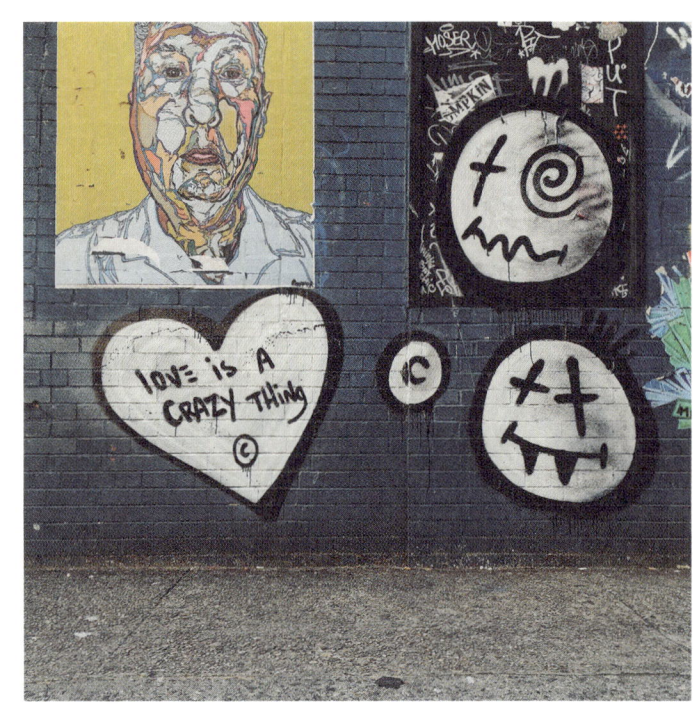

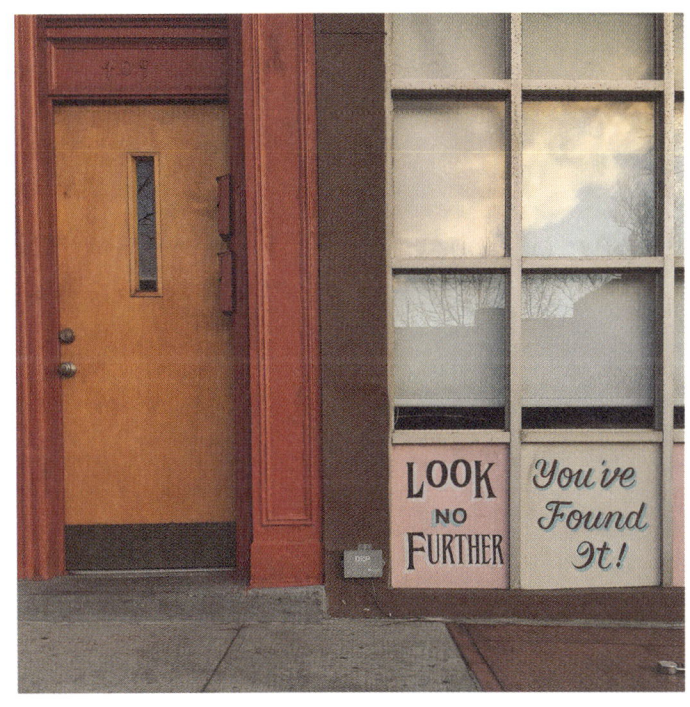
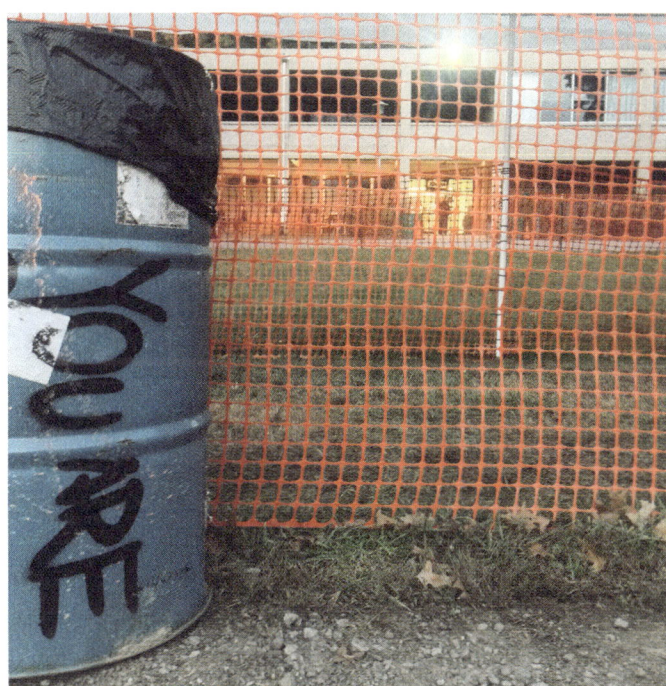

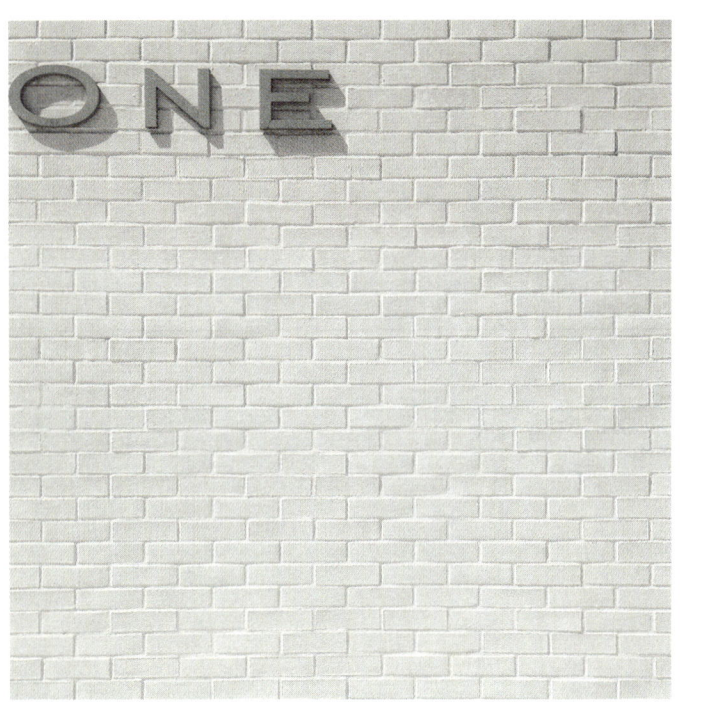
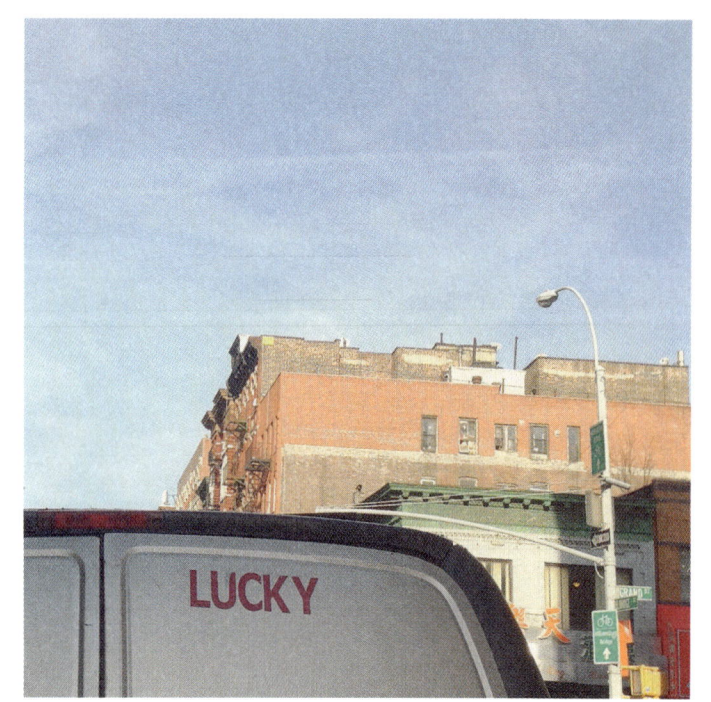

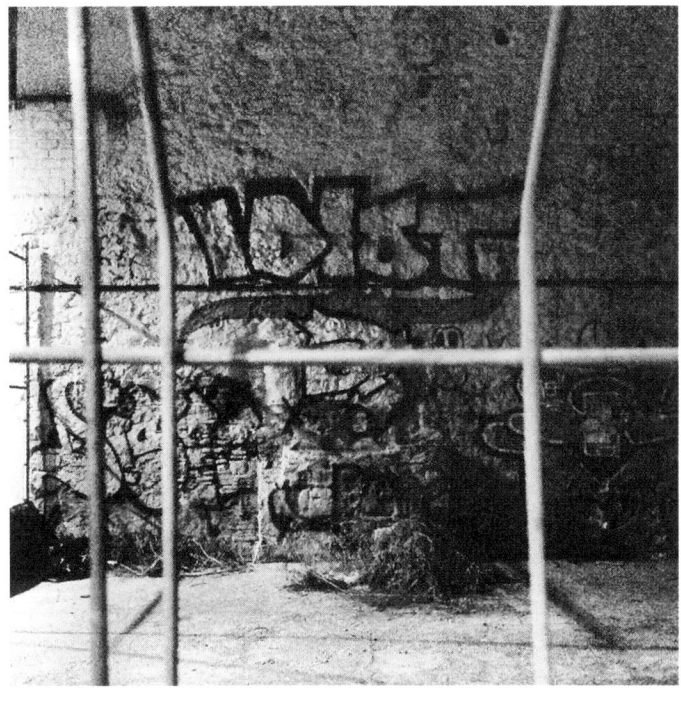

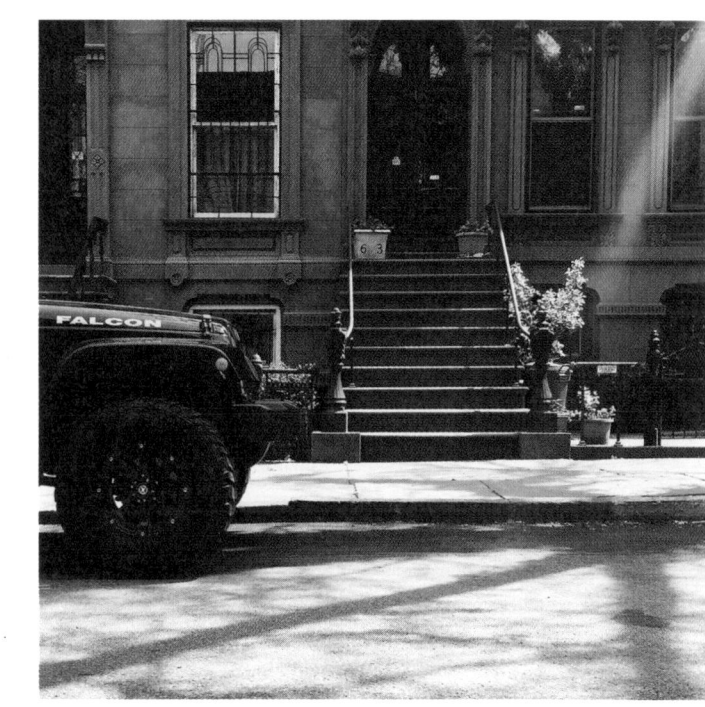

NATURE CHANNEL

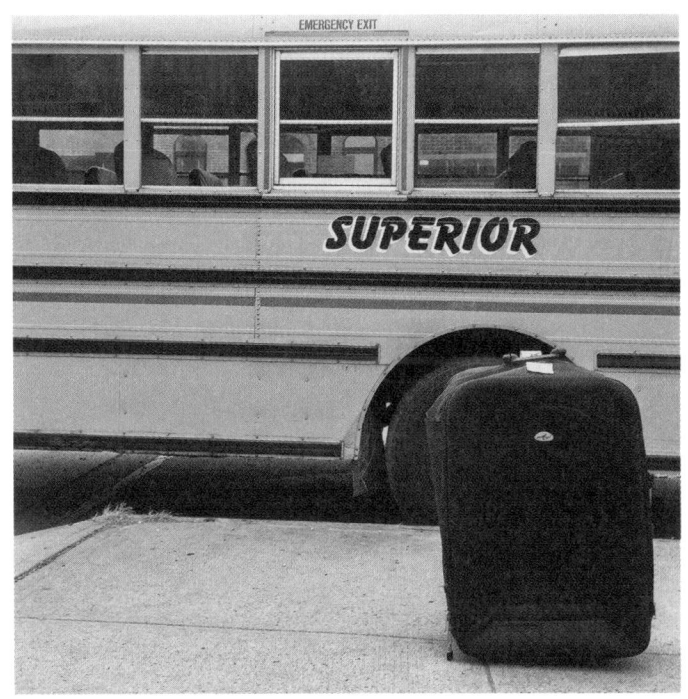
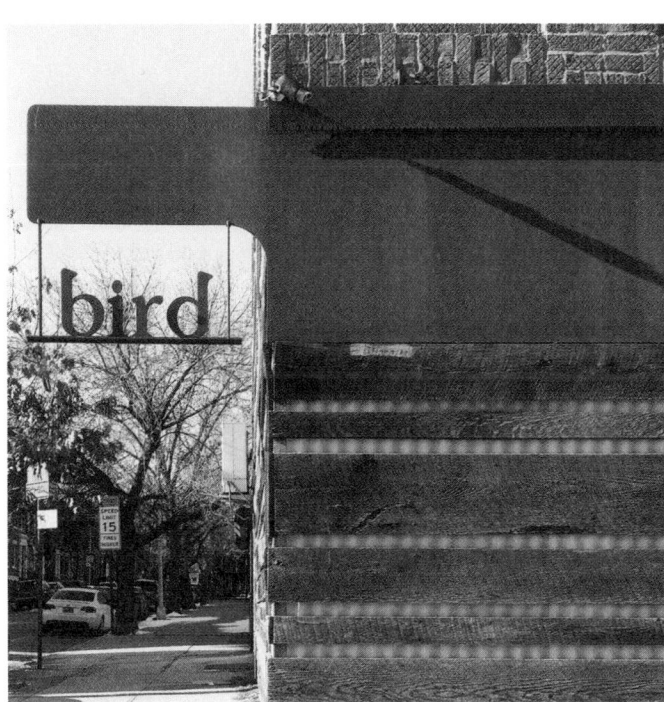

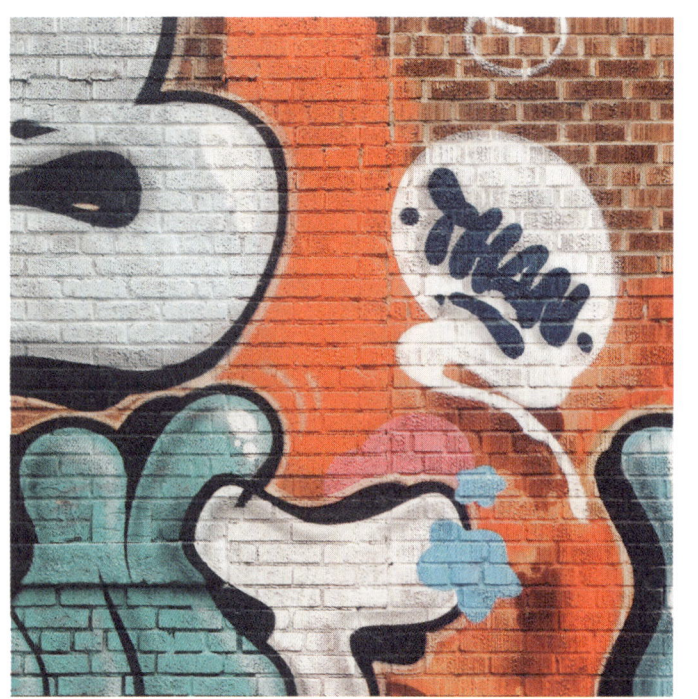
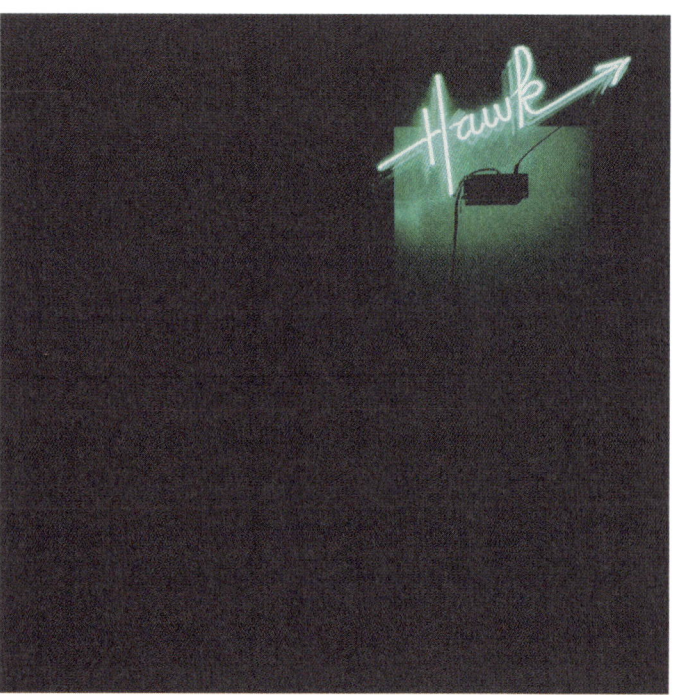

FAIRYTALES

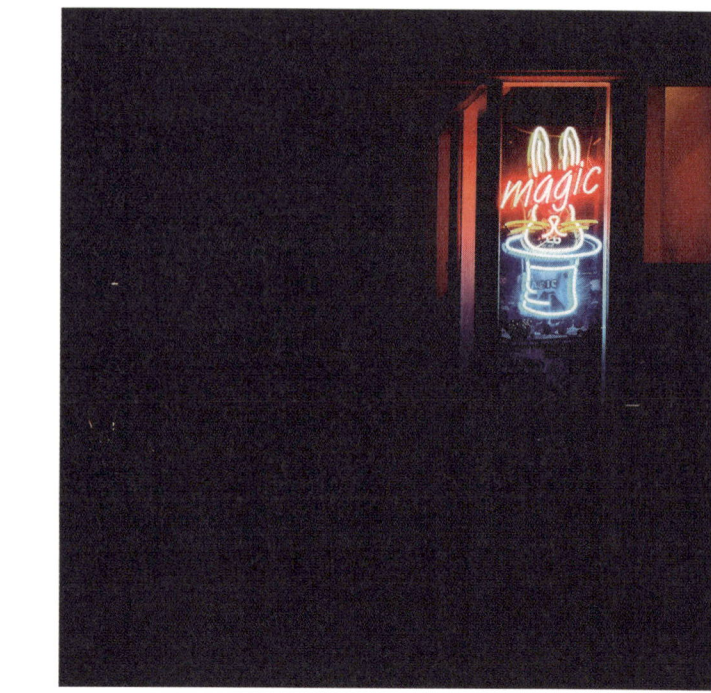

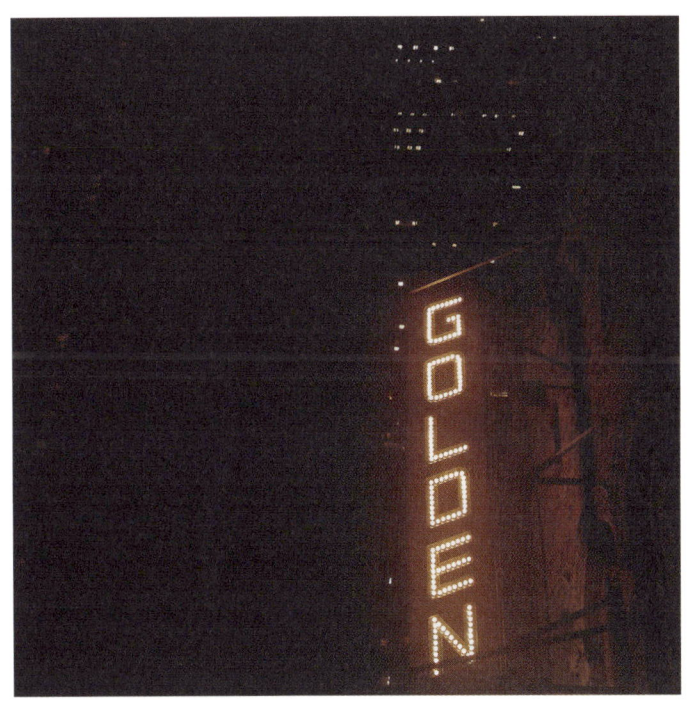
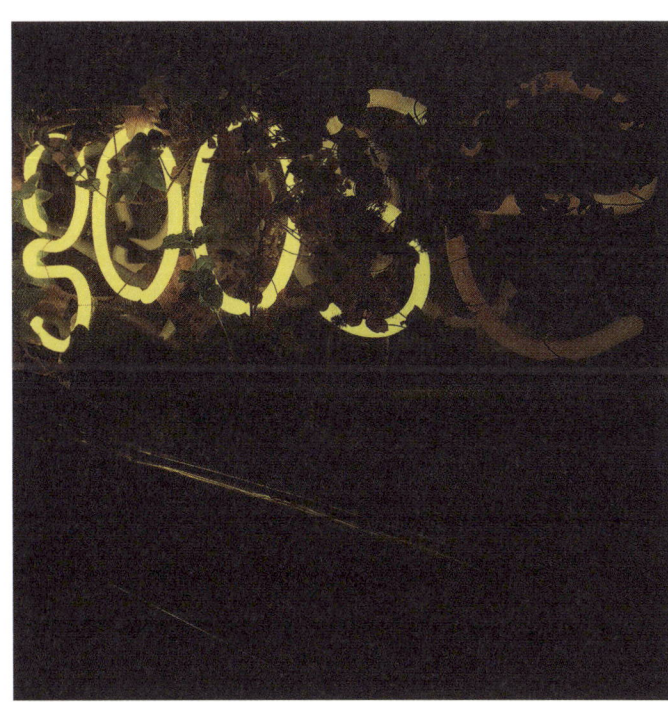

TIME TO RUN

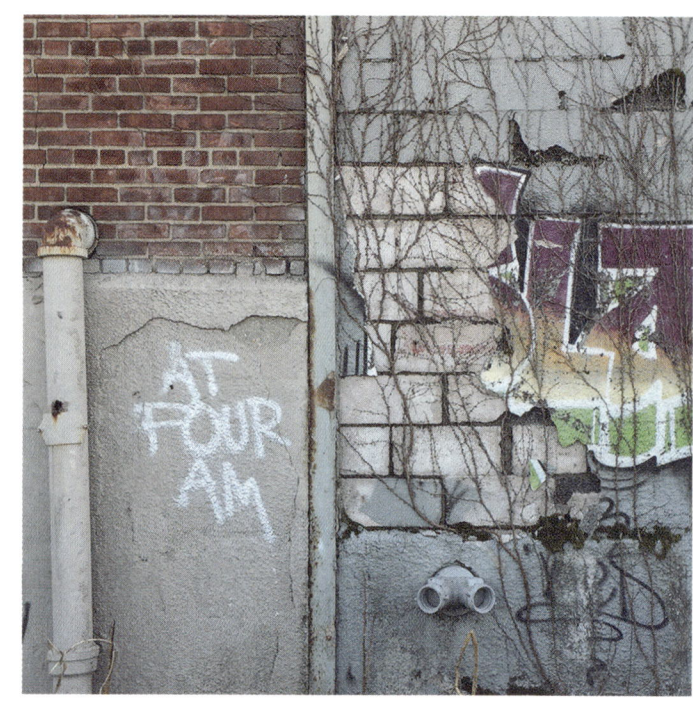

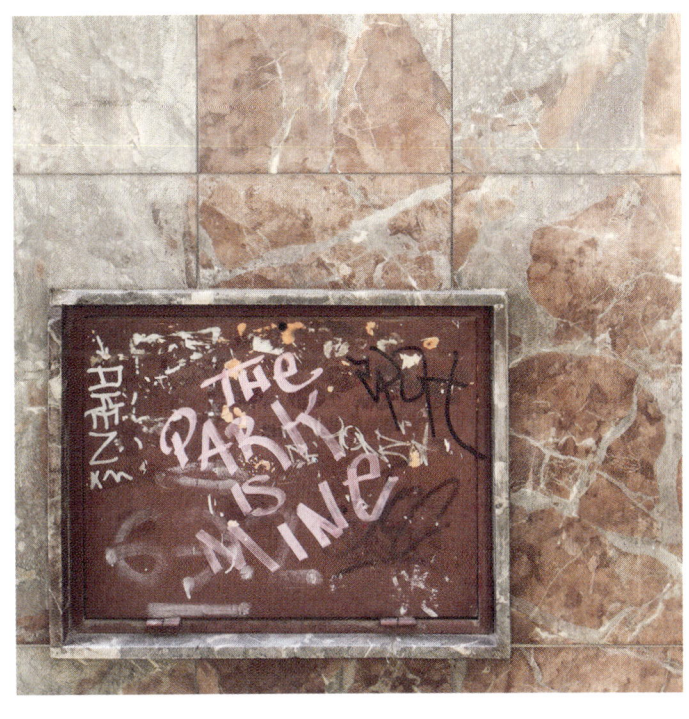

IN THE STREETS

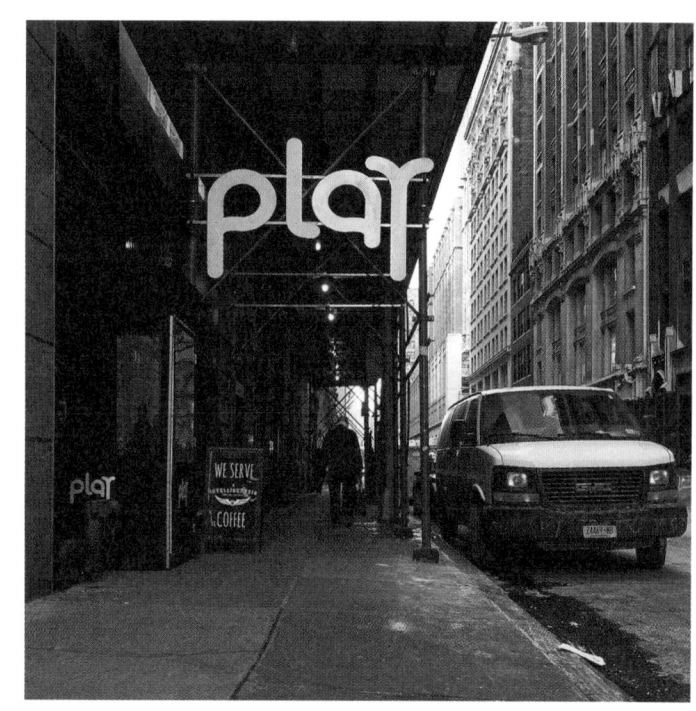

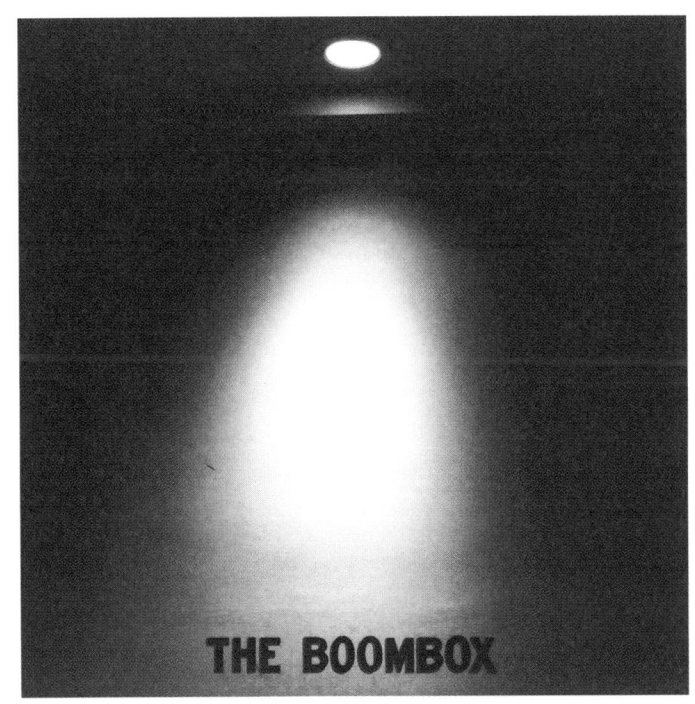

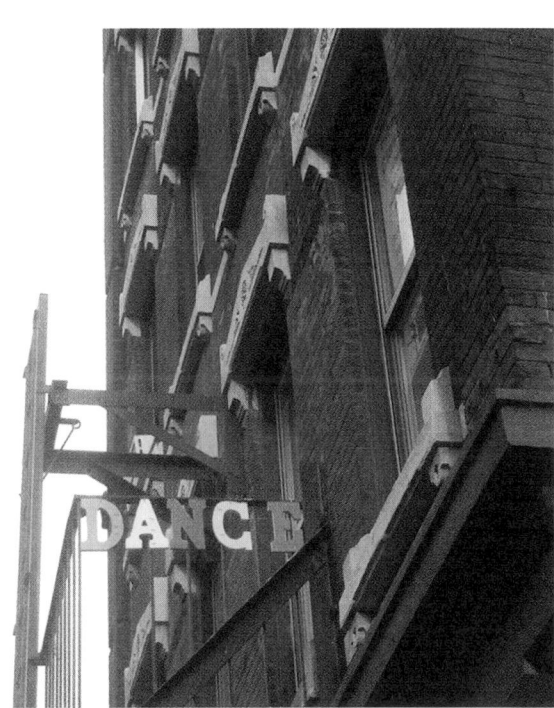

TABLE OF CONTENTS

p. 4 – 5 **It wouldn't flush**
Veterans Bridge | Pittsburgh, PA | 17 September 2014
Louisiana Museum of Modern Art | Humlebæk, Denmark | 22 May 2014
Eco Green Cleaners | Hartsdale, NY | 2 December 2012

p. 6 – 9 **Franks & Beans**
The Hole | New York, NY | 12 August 2014
Goldenshtein Restaurant Equipment | Brooklyn, NY | 8 April 2012
Stortorget | Malmo, Sweden | 21 May 2014
47th Street | Pittsburgh, PA | 14 March 2014

p. 10 – 13 **Knock twice ask for bob**
Chestnut Street | Philadelphia, PA | 22 July 2012
South Elliott Place | Brooklyn, NY | 13 January 2013
Bayardstown Social Club | Pittsburgh, PA | 11 August 2013
Creative Reuse | Pittsburgh, PA | 20 April 2013
Where All the Toys Are | Canonsburg, PA | 8 February 2014

p. 14 – 15 **See me after class**
Larimer School | Pittsburgh, PA | 10 August 2014
Fort Wetherill | Jamestown, RI | 28 July 2014

p. 16 – 19 **Fat & Lazy**
Fossar de les Moreres | Barcelona, Spain | 18 May 2014
One Mile House | New York, NY | 10 June 2014
Allegheny River | Pittsburgh, PA | 5 November 2013
31st Street Bridge | Pittsburgh, PA | 20 April 2014
Braddock Ave | Braddock, PA | 5 July 2014

p. 20 – 21 **Shotgun**
Construction Junction | Pittsburgh, PA | 22 February 2014
Downing Street | Pittsburgh, PA | 6 June 2014
Newport Folk Fest | Newport, RI | 28 July 2012

p. 22 – 25 **When I grow up**
Late Night Stars Deli | Brooklyn, NY | 13 June 2012
Marble Way | Pittsburgh, PA | 8 January 2014
Dream Forge Films | Emsworth, PA | 19 October 2014
Domino Sugar Factory | Brooklyn, NY | 20 January 2015
Broadway Station G Train | Brooklyn, NY | 12 January 2015
Troy Hill | Pittsburgh, PA | 20 March 2014
Porter Avenue | Brooklyn, NY | 20 January 2015

p. 26 – 29 **One eye open**
Butler Street | Pittsburgh, PA | 29 May 2014
Bowery Restaurant Supply | New York, NY | 10 June 2014
Carnegie Robotics | Pittsburgh, PA | 23 February 2014
Bob's Garage | Blawnox, PA | 14 November 2013
Troutman Street | Brooklyn, NY | 20 January 2015

p. 30 – 31 **Chapter one**
Paynes Way | Asheville, NC | 2 April 2014
Metropolitan Station G Train | Brooklyn, NY | 19 May 2012
Avenue A | New York, NY | 28 May 2012

p. 32 – 35 **Freak show**
Marysia Beauty Salon | New York, NY | 18 December 2014
Fat Baby | New York, NY | 17 October 2014

Penn Avenue | Pittsburgh, PA | 22 June 2014
Café Regular | Brooklyn, NY | 13 January 2015
Dogma Church | Pittsburgh, PA | 13 October 2014

p. 36 - 37 **The drunk jockey**
Schenley Park | Pittsburgh, PA | 21 July 2013
Thick Bikes | Pittsburgh, PA | 8 June 2014
Butler Street | Pittsburgh, PA | 2 May 2014

p. 38 - 39 **Revelation**
Who New? | Pittsburgh, PA | 30 March 2013
Union Hall | Brooklyn, NY | 10 February 2013
S Church Street | Georgetown, TX | 10 March 2013

p. 40 - 41 **Just married**
Valley Motel | Pittsburgh, PA | 13 April 2013
Green Village Corporation | Brooklyn, NY | 30 September 2012

p. 42 - 45 **Hand in hand**
Veterans Bridge | Pittsburgh, PA | 17 November 2012
South Elliott Place | Brooklyn, NY | 10 December 2012
Moment Hotel | Copenhagen, Denmark | 22 May 2014
Johnson Avenue | Brooklyn, NY | 3 June 2012
The Mr. Roboto Project | Pittsburgh, PA | 30 July 2013
Haywood Road | Asheville, NC | 2 April 2014

p. 46 - 47 **Gone too soon**
Dean Hotel | Providence, RI | 25 May 2014
Polish Hill | Pittsburgh, PA | 5 June 2014
N 13th Street | Brooklyn, NY | 2 August 2012

p. 48 - 49 **Old & Senile**
Rivington Street | New York, NY | 17 October 2014
East Hartsdale Ave | Hartsdale, NY | 21 January 2013
St. Peter and Paul Parochial School | Pittsburgh, PA | 13 October 2014

p. 50 - 53 **Flipper flipped out**
Meinert Truck & Auto | Pittsburgh, PA | 20 November 2014
Morrison Alley | Boulder, CO | 27 September 2011
Controversy | Pittsburgh, PA | 24 Novemebr 2014
East Sherman Street | Millvale, PA | 22 April 2014
Playa Ciutadella | Barcelona, Spain | 18 May 2014

p. 54 - 59 **Pit stop**
Main Street | Weaverville, NC | 3 April 2014
Berlin Way | Pittsburgh, PA | 2 November 2013
Take A Break Bar | Pittsburgh, PA | 4 May 2014
Farnsworth Art Museum | Rockland, ME | 26 September 2014
Indian Creek Valley Road | Melcroft, PA | 26 June 2014
India Palace Cuisine | Pittsburgh, PA | 7 June 2014
Pleasant Street | Boulder, CO | 19 October 2012
Vilella Sign & Design | New Kensington, PA | 12 March 2014
Pittsburgh Cheese Terminal | Pittsburgh, PA | 24 April 2014
Bayardstown Social Club | Pittsburgh, PA | 21 June 2013

p. 60 - 61 **A request from the queen**
Pearl Street | Boulder, CO | 23 August 2011
Daily Bread | Pittsburgh, PA | 29 April 2014
Hidden Treasures | Braddock, PA | 5 July 2014

p. 62 – 65 **Last goodbye**
33rd Street | Pittsburgh, PA | 14 March 2014
Blackberry Way | Pittsburgh, PA | 20 January 2014
Grant's Block | Providence, RI | 28 December 2013
Tin Town | Georgetown, TX | 22 March 2013
Herrs Island | Pittsburgh, PA | 20 April 2014
Pine Street Church | Boulder, CO | 27 September 2011

p. 66 – 69 **And they're off**
Lucky Fish | New York, NY | 17 October 2014
Belvit Way | Pittsburgh, PA | 11 March 2014
Pittsburgh Filmmakers | Pittsburgh, PA | 3 June 2014
Fort Wetherill | Jamestown, RI | 28 July 2014
The Chair Factory | New York, NY | 17 October 2014

p. 70 – 73 **Chef's special**
Frankies Extra Long | Pittsburgh, PA | 7 December 2013
Manhattan Bridge | New York, NY | 2 December 2014
Brooklyn Hotdogs | Brooklyn, NY | 29 July 2014
Blackbird Tavern | Temecula, CA | 14 September 2014
Splendid | Brooklyn, NY | 13 January 2015
Rough Trade | Brooklyn, NY | 7 July 2012
Anchovies Food & Spirits | Boston, MA | 8 September 2011

p. 74 – 77 **Mind lost**
Carnegie Science Center | Pittsburgh, PA | 4 Septemebr 2014
Your Self Storage | Pittsburgh, PA | 17 November 2014
Jefferson Station L Train | Brooklyn, NY | 21 April 2012

Find Home Furnishings | Brooklyn, NY | 29 July 2014
Yesterday's Bar & Grill | Pittsburgh, PA | 1 June 2014
Foca Restaurant | Brooklyn, NY | 20 January 2015

p. 78 – 81 **Mother's secret**
Morgan Avenue | Brooklyn, NY | 21 March 2012
N 3rd Street | Brooklyn, NY | 2 July 2012
Tri State Antique Center | Canonsburg, PA | 8 February 2014
Fort Wetherill | Jamestown, RI | 28 July 2014
Outback Saloon | Boulder, CO | 6 March 2015

p. 82 – 85 **Cage match**
Clara Macy School | Bellingham, MA | 11 May 2014
Riverfront Trail | Pittsburgh, PA | 19 April 2014
Carrer de l'Almirall Churruca | Barcelona, Spain | 18 May 2014
Friendship Avenue | Pittsburgh, PA | 7 Novemebr 2013
St. Peter and Paul Parochial School | Pittsburgh, PA | 13 October 2014

p. 86 – 89 **I'm just a prince**
Castle Tavern | Pittsburgh, PA | 3 March 2013
Leila Heller Gallery | New York, NY | 4 December 2014
Ridgeway Street | Pittsburgh, PA | 28 August 2014
S 3rd Street | Brooklyn, NY | 1 August 2014
Beloved | Brooklyn, NY | 12 August 2014
Club Café | Pittsburgh, PA | 11 April 2013
Best Pizza | Brooklyn, NY | 22 January 2015

p. 90 – 93 **XOXO**
Jay Street | Brooklyn, NY | 14 June 2014

Mad Madeline's Grill | Temecula, CA | 14 September 2014
Blush | Pittsburgh, PA | 28 September 2013
Belvederes | Pittsburgh, PA | 3 August 2013
Nelty's Flowers | Brooklyn, NY | 20 January 2015
Water Street | Brooklyn, NY | 14 June 2014

p. 94 - 95 **Quitting time**
Protos Pizza | Boulder, CO | 20 September 2011
Day's Warehouse | Asheville, NC | 2 April 2014
AT&T | Pittsburgh, PA | 27 June 2014

p. 96 - 99 **86 years young**
Spring Lounge | New York, NY | 28 October 2012
McDonough's Antiques | Pittsburgh, PA | 16 November 2013
Golden Peaks Milk House | Golden, CO | 10 October 2014
Lucky Laundry | Brooklyn, NY | 13 January 2015
Grossinger's Catskill Resort Hotel | Liberty, NY | 23 January 2015
S 6th Street | Brooklyn, NY | 20 January 2015
Drop Off Service | New York, NY | 18 December 2014

p. 100 - 101 **Escaping reality**
Dundas Castle | Roscoe, NY | 23 January 2015
N 1st Street | Brooklyn, NY | 20 January 2015
AP Cafe | Brooklyn, NY | 20 January 2015

p. 102 - 105 **A night in love**
S 5th Street | Brooklyn, NY | 20 January 2015
Tease Hair Group | New York, NY | 18 December 2014
Unicorn | New York, NY | 8 January 2015

Brooklyn Navy Yard | Brooklyn, NY | 13 June 2014
D&Y Trading | Brooklyn, NY | 20 January 2015
The Ritz | Boulder, CO | 8 May 2011

p. 106 - 109 **Summer in Russia**
Olde Good Things | New York, NY | 30 December 2013
Boulder Creek Fair | Boulder, CO | 28 September 2011
Three Rivers Heritage Trail | Pittsburgh, PA | 4 November 2014
Sun Oil Company | Blawnox, PA | 4 July 2014
Grossinger's Catskill Resort Hotel | Liberty, NY | 23 January 2015

p. 110 - 113 **Bunkmates**
Camp | Brooklyn, NY | 8 January 2015
Pal's | Johnson City, TN | 3 April 2014
Hotel California | Santa Monica, CA | 12 September 2014
Matthews Palmer Playground | New York, NY | 16 April 2015
Remedy | Pittsburgh, PA | 21 October 2014

p. 114 - 115 **Love, Mom**
Central Parking System | Brooklyn, NY | 9 January 2015
Montrose Ave | Brooklyn, NY | 20 January 2015
Excellent Home Care Services | Brooklyn, NY | 1 August 2014

p. 116 - 119 **Sleep tight**
Bang Bang | New York, NY | 4 December 2014
Kent Avenue | Brooklyn, NY | 20 January 2015
Anotheroom | New York, NY | 16 April 2015
Greenleaf Park | Boulder, CO | 15 March 2015
Guckert Harry Company | Pittsburgh, PA | 19 November 2014

Carrer d'Astúries | Barcelona, Spain | 13 May 2014
Canonsburg Antique Mall | Canonsburg, PA | 15 February 2014

p. 120 – 123 **Lunch lady revenge**
Stagg Street | Brooklyn, NY | 20 January 2015
Troutman Street | Brooklyn, NY | 20 January 2015
Cadi Restaurant | Barcelona, Spain | 14 May 2014
George's Pizza House | Harwich Port, MA | 25 May 2014
Williamsburg Bridge | Brooklyn, NY | 20 January 2015

p. 124 – 127 **Future fears**
Alleghany River | Pittsburgh, PA | 5 November 2013
N 1st Street | Brooklyn, NY | 6 July 2013
The End Is Near | Brooklyn, NY | 13 January 2015
Three Rivers Heritage Trail | Pittsburgh, PA | 4 November 2014
Plaça de Catalunya | Barcelona, Spain | 13 May 2014
Bouldin Creek | Austin, TX | 13 March 2013

p. 128 – 131 **On Broadway**
Cora's Coffee Shoppe | Santa Monica, CA | 15 September 2014
W 13th Street | New York, NY | 23 July 2013
Java Street | Brooklyn, NY | 22 January 2015
36th Street | Pittsburgh, PA | 9 March 2014
Bergen Street | Brooklyn, NY | 9 January 2015
Shine | Cambridge, MA | 15 January 2015

p. 132 – 135 **At first site**
Billymark's West | New York, NY | 8 January 2015
Smith Street Tattoo Parlour | Brooklyn, NY | 5 January 2015

Dixmont State Hospital | Emsworth, PA | 11 October 2014
Shutters on the Beach | Santa Monica, CA | 15 September 2014
Invisible Exports | NewYork, NY | 4 December 2014
Barri Gòtic | Barcelona, Spain | 16 May 2014

p. 136 – 139 **Nature channel**
South Elliott Place | Brooklyn, NY | 19 April 2014
Superior Bus Services | Brooklyn, NY | 21 December 2014
Bird | Brooklyn, NY | 8 January 2015
Chrystie Street | New York, NY | 10 June 2014
Hawk Studios & Gallery | Pittsburgh, PA | 21 September 2013

p. 140 – 141 **Fairytales**
Cuckoo's Nest | Pittsburgh, PA | 28 October 2014
Golden Theater | New York, NY | 4 December 2014
Goose Tattoo | Brooklyn, NY | 12 January 2015

p. 142 – 143 **Time to run**
India Street | Brooklyn, NY | 22 January 2015
Carrer de Sardenya | Barcelona, Spain | 14 May 2014

p. 144 – 145 **In the streets**
Play | New York, NY | 8 Janury 2015
The Boombox | Providence, RI | 27 December 2014
Bagelsmith | Brooklyn, NY | 14 April 2012

BIO

Brian Fouhy is an award winning art director and digital concept creator who has grown an international following with his efforts to transform the internet into one big friendly neighbourhood with a spectrum of imaginative endeavours. Injecting all of his work with a generous shot of humour, Fouhy offers a unique take from behind the viewfinder of his prolific imagination. Brian currently resides in Boulder, Colorado and travels extensively.

Collecting Words is his first book.

Published by New Heroes & Pioneers
Photography and text by Brian Fouhy
Edited by Francois Le Bled
Creative Direction by Jens Lennartsson
Book design by Anna Goffe
Printed and bound by K-print (Estonia)

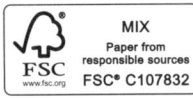

FSC MIX Paper from responsible sources FSC® C107832
www.fsc.org

Legal deposit October 2015
ISBN 978-91-87815-90-4

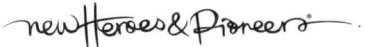